Born in Guyana to immigrant parents and dubbed a most Anglo-Saxon name, compliments of aspirational norms, Karen Ann Vinh, now Flynn, was raised in a West Indian environment; a culture of harsh truths, no-nonsense parenting, and brutish competition at all levels from the playground to the classroom. Karen recognized her strength as a young woman to look at situations from an impartial viewpoint and her ability to be straightforward and honest. From early jobs to becoming a successful entrepreneur, Karen worked toward a fulfilling and resonant life by pursuing things that made her "feel." After working for several international communication agencies, Karen developed her own, to deliver a high quality of work for clients which matched the integrity she felt was required for brands. Within two years of setting up her agency in January 2009, she found a suitor in the fourth largest (at that time)

global communication group who eventually bought her firm in 2016. Karen then dedicated her craft and passion to charities in the UK, where she completed her training as a professional coach. Now at home in Vancouver, Canada, Karen continues to embody and advocate living a larger and fulfilling life through her work to impact inclusion for the growing migrant population arriving in Canada. Karen provides coaching and mentorship for private clients internationally, entrepreneurs, and business students at the University of British Columbia (UBC), and through non-profit organizations in the Vancouver area.

This book is dedicated to my greatest champion, my amazing daughter, who has shown me the true meaning of unconditional love and support. Without you, my darling, my wings could not reach their full span and I love you in the most absolute way I never dreamed possible. You continue to be the brightest star in my sky.

Coach K

GO BEYOND RESILIENCE

FIND YOUR GRIT

AUSTIN MACAULEY PUBLISHERS™

LONDON • CAMBRIDGE • NEW YORK • SHARJAH

Copyright © Coach K (2019)

Ordering Information:
Quantity sales: special discounts are available on quantity purchases by corporations, associations, and others. For details, contact the publisher at the address below.

Publisher's Cataloging-in-Publication data
K, Coach
Go Beyond Resilience: Find Your Grit

ISBN 9781643787510 (Paperback)
ISBN 9781643787527 (Hardback)
ISBN 9781645365068 (ePub e-book)

Library of congress Control number: 2019907840

The main category of the book — Biography & Autobiography / General

www.austinmacauley.com/us

First Published (2019)
Austin Macauley Publishers LLC
40 Wall Street, 28th Floor
New York, NY 10005
USA

mail-usa@austinmacauley.com
+1(646)5125767

I am deeply grateful for the people who have made a great impact on my life in my first half-century. Friends across the globe who have become my family, providing unwavering love and support; excellent bosses in various organizations who trusted me and gave me the opportunities to do new things my way; and my clients and mentees who share their journeys and give me permission to challenge them in order to explore new perspectives and hold themselves accountable.

To Peter Elston – thank you. I learned a great deal about myself during our years together.

Prologue

This book is a result of many years of reflection on my fifty-year journey so far, through failures and successes personally and professionally. My introduction to coaching some years ago made me acutely aware of the deeper feelings I was writing about in my dozens of journals – which I pull out of carefully sealed boxes every time I move through continents.

My unique upbringing in an Asian household on the edge of South America, in a West Indian culture, embroidered the threads that formed me from two very distinct parental backgrounds – each parent Asian, but with opposing ideas on parenting and how they demonstrate affection. I am probably one of the most multi-cultured people I know in a single human being, coming from such a colorful canvas, and furthermore, traveling the world and living in many different countries in my first half-century.

My career in communication was rich and filled me with satisfaction. I had the amazing experience to work with teams of people across many different countries and cultures, and I received invaluable lessons in human behavior. As a young woman launching myself into adulthood, life, and embracing every new adventure, I recognized that I was going to continue to decorate the fabric of my DNA with new experiences. Each year I play the movie "My Life So Far" and reflect on the risks I am taking when I am blossoming and what is holding me back.

Knowing that I was resilient as a child and young woman came relatively early, I clearly had the bravery to make difficult and unpopular decisions throughout my first half-century, and I developed a tenacity and grit that went beyond resilience which stemmed from striving for a better life. I have used the help of counseling and coaching to dissect my thoughts and some deep regrets over time. At various stages, the different types of support have been instrumental in moving my thinking forward to give me the motivation I needed and in some cases, a really hard kick on the backside.

I am grateful for the remarkable friendships I have – men and women, who over the years have given me support, love, and immeasurable kindness. I continuously strive to ensure we feed each other the same way and I will carry these deep connections in my heart forever. The greatest lesson I have learned is that living a full life must include resolute friendships and laughter. There is no other remedy for your soul than a friend who understands and connects with you in a way that feels like you are parts of one – each conversation fills your heart and you genuinely love every difference and every similarity in this stranger.

My partners who have shared large chunks of my life have made a deep impact and I carry no resentment whatsoever that we are divorced. I am stronger and more aware of what I love about life as a result of their presence.

And finally, from witnessing all the trends in mindfulness, chasing dreams, being unapologetic, authentic living, practicing good virtues, and all the rest, none of our goals and dreams would be possible without personal strength and drive to make it happen. My hope is that more people see the necessity in risk and take each situation one at a time. There will be huge pitfalls and mistakes made. However, along the way we become braver and more knowledgeable about the richness in living, rather than letting our lives simply go by.

The Flux of Love
and Loathing

What an incredible sequence of events the last few years! Uncomfortable holidays and weekends, including memorable trips to exotic locations around the world at great expense – my daughter in all her glory as a beautiful young woman finding her way; myself, feeling desperately trapped in my environment and in my skin, with the occasional walk-about in my head. And the saddest part, I was in my second marriage that was only two years old when these painful sensations started to land with a thump in my chest.

I wanted to run away and flee from my life, my marriage and my home; at the same time, I felt this deep-rooted sense of responsibility, guilt, and hate for myself that I could be so stupid. Aren't second marriages supposed to be the smart choice? Didn't I consider this very carefully and all its merits before taking the leap? I felt like a fool and a fraud. I had tricked my brain into a false sense of security. I was in love with the fact that I had found a fun companion to live with and to go on holidays together.

What unfolded since those intense emotions bubbled to the surface has been like a movie – sometimes in slow motion, and at other times, quite an action-packed blur past my eyes. My brain has gone into overload so many times that I lost count – I have to stop myself from reaching for the Advance Panadol to dull the physical pain. The sheer sadness of my situation led me to think of ways to move on and push the restart button.

The home I felt so proud of became a deep freeze – living in it a surreal experience as I went about my days, my two doggies my constant companion. I lived for a year in a zombie state, showing little emotion and saying even less to my husband. It was like no other experience I've had or wish to have ever again. Sadly, I held disdain and downright despised myself for making another mistake when I should have been certain that my second chapter would be starting over "correctly."

We've all been at hard crossroads and some make decisions instinctively, while others ponder and pose, and find it a painful process to even begin. To make a decision means pointing yourself in one direction, committing, and being ready to face whatever comes with that decision. Correct?

Some of us, by delaying a decision, in itself a decision, allow the guilt and pain in our hearts to bubble like thick lava. We feel that stifling our happiness and joy is a price we must pay instead of upsetting the sense of wellbeing for people around us. In many personal situations, I've witnessed this existence – sadness takes over at our core and we think it's better than the options we clearly have but refuse to acknowledge. But consider this – what type of person are you when you are crushed by sadness and neglect? What sort of parent do you become? If you're unable to love yourself by facing positive alternatives, how can you possibly love anyone around you?

What have my hard crossroads taught me? The power and determination to self-assess and answer hard truths about myself is a gift that I am most grateful for – it served me in the past and will continue to serve me extremely well now and in the future. One of the hardest part is accepting the journey ahead, the changes that are necessary, which often cause discomfort for people close to us. Once I imagined what those changes should be, then it was an easier step to determine the course of action. It may well sound robotic but then going into survival mode and doing what is necessary to separate one's life from a partner and physically moving to a different continent is similar, in my mind, to a military operation or setting up a new business venture. It is a course of action that needs care and precision and good planning. I am not a cold person but I know what I want in life and I am fully prepared to get it.

None of this is easy. But it's easier than living in a deep freeze…suspended with no emotion in a place that is supposed to be home, a haven, my and our oasis. Living with all feelings and desires shoved aside and never allowed to bubble and be fulfilled is brutal and cruel. This brutality extends to the most basic form of intimacy…none of it acknowledged, cherished, or satisfied. To say that my back was firmly against the wall would be a gross understatement and I knew myself well; this could fling me into therapy again, or I could close my eyes and remember all the things I am supposed to do if I were being honest with my feelings and set my intentions to be happy and content. I decided to close my eyes...

Building Blocks

I was born and raised in a tiny and, one might say, insignificant blot on the South American continent. In the shadow of Venezuela and Brazil, my tiny country has the great claim to fame of Reverend Jim Jones who poisoned over nine hundred of his disciples including children with cyanide-laced Koolaid. More prestigiously, the glorious Amazon Forest cuts across our country's interior, giving us an amazing diversity of rivers, wildlife, natural minerals, and waterfalls.

As a Guyanese, I was born into a minority family. My mother was mixed East Indian and Portuguese, born from plantation workers who somehow managed to make their way from Madras, India, to Guyana, South America. I still haven't figured that one out. My father, a more adventurous and even sensational story... Fleeing the French conflict in the 1920s, he made it onto a fishing trawler with a group of friends and fled Hanoi, Vietnam, to travel across the high seas before finally settling on the upper corner edge off the South American continent – first Suriname, then French Guiana, then British Guiana (which became independent Guyana in 1965).

I remember my father telling me how many lands they touched, before deciding to get off that trawler for good.

Despite not knowing the full details, I am immensely proud of the sheer grit and determination that my father held in him.

If anything, my determination and commitment to a course of action and its destination, whatever it may be, comes directly through my father's genes. I can feel it in my bones. When I decide I'm going to do something, watch out, here I come.

Over my first half-century, I have faced adversity in varying degrees of severity. Sometimes I thought I would just crawl under a rock for months. I have and I did for short periods of time, but eventually, I talked myself into action for the greater good of me. My friends have played a significant role in getting me out from under rocks. However, first and foremost, it has been my sheer grit and determination to be a good person and an amazing mother which drove me to flick my saboteurs off my shoulders, take a deep breath, stand two inches taller, and put a brave foot in front the other.

I didn't wait to be rescued nor did I get to the point of critical self-harm. I have indulged in self-harm with alcohol and drugs, and frankly, it felt great at the time, but I just don't have the ability to say "give up." My intentions, which I set for myself as a human being and as a mother, empowered me with the hunger to succeed and fulfill the destiny I set for myself. To many, this sounds horrendously corny but it's my truth. I examined my needs and wants early on in life and I know what makes my pulse race and what kills my soul. I believe everyone has that ability – to examine and face what brings them joy and contentment and pursue it in a smart way to minimize emotional and collateral damage.

I was a very bright child. I stood in my father's shop making change for customers without the use of a cash register or calculator – the days of commerce in Guyana in the early 1970s was bare bones. My father's shop consisted of the wares we sold, in glass cases scattered around the shop space, and a counter behind which we stood smiling at customers – our cash box and drawers safely behind us. My brain fired like a computer when I was seven years old, my parents proudly showing off my mathematics skills to everyone, who hesitated by the way, when they looked down at this short kid behind the counter handling money and making change.

From a very young age, I observed people – it brought me great joy to just watch them. I stood in that shop and took it all in…people coming and going, what and how they spoke to each other, when they didn't communicate, the things that made them angry and how they reacted, fights that broke out in our neighborhood, and general attitudes and moods amongst neighbors. Our shop was busy, as it was perched on a busy corner where two main streets intersected. And there was a very popular "rum shop" across the street from us. It was a gathering place that was immensely social during paycheck days…that invariably added to the color and activities at that intersection.

I remember having "street smarts" very early on. Living in a third world country, it was vital to know how to avoid pickpockets and to not look like an easy target for burglars and bullies. I even tried different words on people to get varied results – testing my communication power on unsuspecting teenagers and adults around me. I got into fistfights as a seven and eight-year-old, negotiating overzealously with friends when we played competitive games. Sometimes not pretty, but I was and I still am quite competitive.

My determination has given me wings – it also made me impatient with studying and sitting at a desk in school. I loathed teachers who favored the bright kids and spent little time trying to grasp why other children needed more of an explanation. In fact, I was a horrible student. From around nine years old, right through to high school – fourteen years old – I did everything I could to irritate teachers I didn't like and to fill my classroom with laughter. Yes, indeed I was a class clown! You wouldn't guess that now by looking at me – I'm told I am a rather serious, intimidating woman these days. I actually look into a mirror once in a while (briefly) and smile at myself, convincing myself for a few minutes that I am not intimidating.

I did extremely well in the early days and even skipped a grade going straight from Primary Three to Five. When it was time to take the Common Entrance Examination to move into high school, I was nine years old. The average age was typically eleven years for a child taking the exam to decide which high school they would spend the next five years in order to take the GCSE examinations, followed by A Levels. Yes, Guyana was an English frontier and our education system remains steeped in the British system, which is a point of pride for parents.

I suppose it was around my fourteenth birthday that I decided I was too smart, too impatient, and too driven to stay on the straight and narrow course. I rebelled badly (in addition to being a jokester in class) and unexpectedly, so no one saw it coming. My parents had split up when I was ten years old and I had been living in a haze since – in a suspended state, just moving from days to days, routinely following the physical needs for shelter, food, and expectations from teachers at school. Moving into my sister's house without any choice in the matter, I was treated like a live-in servant. I didn't mind; it kept me very busy and I was happy not being a family member. I had a handful of great friends at school and I loved nothing more than hanging out with them every chance I had outside of classes. That was the beginning of "my friends, my tribe, my village."

Along with my determination to be a successful human being (even before I hit fourteen years old), I decided that I would never marry a West Indian man. Don't ask me where that came from. I just knew and I fixed it in my head that I would explore the world, find a man that could be my partner instead of one that expected me to serve him hand and foot, and one that had a light touch when it came to living on this planet. I found during my life in Guyana, which is considered West Indian because of our culture, our footprint was heavy; we had little regard for the environment, other people, or anything else outside our own shadows.

My very first taste of freedom, spreading my wings, and looking at opportunities full-on was the day I landed in the British Virgin Islands with a couple of suitcases for a seventeen-day vacation to visit my sister. She had made Tortola her new home to escape her abusive West Indian husband and was enjoying a new lease on life. I took one look at the island and knew that with some maneuvering and smart planning, I could turn this into my future. It was to be and I never looked back at Guyana.

I took it upon myself to meet people on the tiny island – who knew who, who could help me establish a new life, who I could work for and with to impress; it was another practical life lesson which pushed and expanded me further. I didn't even know this was networking at its very best. I loved the challenge and I thrived on it.

After my tourist visa ran out, with no chance of another renewal, I went to see the man high up in government on the tiny island of Tortola and presented my case to him – not just to extend my visa but to grant me residency on the island. I think I was so brazen that he just sat there not believing this young woman – presenting my capabilities and potential much like a business plan. I was nineteen years old and I didn't hesitate for one moment. I booked the appointment, went in, and presented my case. I set bold intentions and I got exactly what I hoped for.

Within weeks, I had landed a very nice job and was proving myself to be a great asset in an office environment. I was hardworking and used my initiative to make two insurance agents' lives a whole lot better. Their clients shouted my praise and before long, I was invaluable to them and known in the community. I was very proud of myself and it was the start of my deep and life-long interest in the field of marketing and communication.

The Strength of a Child

In essence, my earliest memory is probably when I was around three or four years old – in my father's shop. As I observed customers come in and go out, listening to their banter, bicker, and general goings-on in the busy little retail shop, my thoughts were formed.

I remember my mother waking at the crack of dawn to get things ready to open shop, busily serving customers from 7 am till 9 pm. My father in and out all day – driving off to buy new products for the glass cases, putting out the cash kitty in the till each morning, and counting the money each night before deciding how much to hide away. It was an era that is emblazoned in my brain forever, plus the picture of a nutty, skewed role for man and woman.

Once I was old enough, I was given various tasks to do around the shop. To my father, my mother and I were the staff. We all had our roles, and truthfully, the parts fit and it worked. I refilled items in the fridge, washed things, swept the floor, and got handed down jobs as seen fit by my mother. I went to school, played outside with my friends, and worked in the shop. Of course, now that I look back at this incredible experience, it was the nuts and bolts of my entrepreneur in the making. I witnessed how business was done and sucked in the knowledge I gathered from watching people day in and day out – handling cash and understanding the value of sales, relevant products, and good service for profit. Uncanny and real – it all stuck with me.

Like my parents, I lived and breathed that shop, from seven in the morning when I opened my eyes, to the last thing at night when I collapsed in bed (my school hours aside, which I loved). My mother was very resentful that the shop was her only existence and she felt a slave to it. My father, on the other hand, the business head in the equation, was delighted that his shop was a successful business in the community. We had an enviable location and super busy footpath – yep, even at eight years old my brain registered this… He was in charge of the strategy and supplies, and she was the master at operations. I made the mental note to myself to be a boss, not slave. The seed to being an entrepreneur was sown…!

I believe people from many different backgrounds have valuable lessons peppered throughout their lives like I did. However, while some actually dissect the situations and outcome and imprint the learning into their brain, many others box up incidents and accidents into distant and past memories. They think lightly of why, what, and how these situations could actually be pivotal points in their thinking, and the way in which they pursue goals and fulfillment.

If you could write down the three most memorable incidents in your life so far, what would they be? And what are the greatest takeaways you've ignored in the way you live today?

I remember having playtime with children in our neighborhood. We climbed neighbors' trees and picked fresh fruit, rolled marbles in the dirt, played hide-and-seek around the houses and yards for half a mile, traded rubber bands, played hop scotch and jump rope, and sometimes we made wooden cars and other toys like kites with our bare hands and with materials gathered from the streets. My playtime was fantastic and I remember loving the satisfaction of making things from scrap. Toys that actually worked and had moving parts, we raced our go-karts and cars which we made – me and a bunch of Guyanese/West Indian children at ages six to eight years old. All of us were of various colors and socio-economic backgrounds and all happy-go-lucky when we were out in the big yards playing away from the scrutiny of our parents who were all severely strict.

Getting outside to play with friends was the highlight of my days. It felt like freedom from prison every time I went outside "the shop." Between school, my chores in my father's shop, and limited playtime with friends, I felt consumed. I look back at my childhood like a black-and-white movie and it was full of hard work. Highlights were great and joyful, but short-lived. During the long school holidays, I remember my mother having to come and find me. Invariably, I would forget that after 6 pm I should be heading home. This led to my mother being supremely cross and if she was in a bad mood, a smack landed across my head. Another West Indian trait I could never reconcile…hitting kids, hard, to communicate something. I wouldn't call it discipline. It never really instilled any valuable lessons in any of the kids I knew were hit, including me. Instead, we all hated it and looked at our parents like they were bullies.

Sometime after my eighth birthday, things really started to go south...more yelling and screaming at home, more outings by my mother who stayed out longer and came back stinking of rum and more trips overseas by my father. Things crumbled faster and finally just before my tenth birthday, their separation happened, talking through lawyers, decision on my living arrangements being made as if I were a piece of furniture, and a lot of unhappiness and sadness consumed the bustling home I had known as a small girl.

There was no positive way for me as a child to look at this. My home was being torn apart. My mother was going her way and demanding money from my father; my father was planning his exit from the country and hiding whatever finances he could from her. My sister, herself in a loveless and violent marriage, was burdened with her ten-year-old sister in a two-bedroom house where she already had two sons. Christ, could you imagine anything worse?

Now, with the strength of hindsight and a somewhat-grown-up perspective on all that happened during that period of my life, I examine the way in which things stuck with me and taught me enormous lessons. That hopelessness at the time felt like the deepest canyon, but now, I can see just how much reflection I did. Unfortunately, I sat in my classroom doing just that. Teachers thought I was daydreaming, but I spent countless hours in high school between the ages of eleven to fourteen years old just imagining how I could make the best of such a situation.

Although I knew that my education was important, I also considered that I needed to be realistic. A plan of action was required, with hard goals. I needed to set my intentions in order to progress into a life that would be my own, and at a quick pace. Till today, I consider it a vital part of life to be utterly honest with oneself, one's circumstances, and look at realistic outcomes one small step at a time. To understand our strengths and to adapt to challenges is a skill that many people have, but few take the bold action to secure the life they dream of. Striving for significant change, improving quality of life, and feeling safe is not a gift; it's what we owe ourselves. There is no life worth living if it's underneath us. The days we spend in our heads and around loved ones deserve our best selves. We deserve our best selves to be happy and content.

The shock of my family disintegrating before my eyes led me to think of what I would not tolerate in my own adult life; the suffering of relatives close to me instilled my promise to myself to find happiness and surround myself with positive, non-violent people. The misguided priorities which led to deep discontentment in the adults around me taught me a remarkable lesson about life's goals and achievements.

I look back at my first fifteen years and reflect on the strengths and attributes that showed up early. I didn't have a full childhood – I had to grow up fast, and I learned to be capable and self-reliant. I could do things a six or eight-year-old should not be competent doing at that age.

Children should be good at playing and making a mess. Well, I observed and learned from human behavior, body language, choice of words, aggression, fake compassion, and the good and the ugly... All of it sunk in like ink into my skin and my brain. It made me sure of what I did not want – for myself, in myself, and in the people I would choose to be with. Having such black and white separation of wants and walls, I suppose, formed me both adversely and positively.

In the long run, I might have developed the inability to give people a whole lot of time to prove themselves, and over the years, I have moved on too quickly in some instances. Yes, I've made mistakes when it came to judging people too quickly – showing a lack of tolerance or acceptance for differences. Like so much in life, hindsight serves well. A good dash at current age tells us what we should have, could have, and might have done differently.

I am blessed and grateful for all the learning. While I am not grateful for not having a full childhood, I like the fact I am self-sufficient and able to look at things for what they are. It gave me the ability to be frank, open, and face fears with stamina. Facing adversity with bravery is highly underrated, I feel. While I fully appreciate the need for vulnerability from time to time, strength is needed every day to live a full life.

What Do You Mean
"the Formative Years?"

The years that followed my family home falling apart were filled with hurt and cunning. It took every bit of strength then as a ten-year-old to survive the waves of shock and reality that came afterwards. My survival instinct developed acutely and effectively to protect me. In fact, thinking back to various situations and my reactions, while I worked hard to protect myself, it seemed to be well within my capability early on. Of course I made poor decisions as a young adolescent but I honed my instinct, and I also made very brave decisions. My reflexes, or innate sense of survival coupled with entrepreneurial ingenuity to see the bigger picture, motivated me to work towards that. I sat in classes picturing my life on a screen in front of my face. Of course, the fact that I was building these reflexes up constantly throughout my childhood and my adolescence meant that my decision-making was heavily influenced by what was going on in my gut and my head – together. Now, I can appreciate that emotional intelligence and just how powerfully my gut spoke to me.

I was building survivor's instinct instead of being a child. I was maneuvering and manipulating my way around wicked and unconscionable adults instead of going to school and learning and developing as a healthy young woman. However, while I missed out on childhood laughter and innocence, I gained a tremendous gift in understanding and trusting my emotional intelligence and my intuition.

My relatives, including my parents, left me fending for myself far too young. At fourteen years of age, I ended up fending for them, the adults. I tried in the end to look at my mother's face with compassion when she was gravely ill, and it was hard. When she passed away, I was relieved. I was completely unprepared for boys and my high school experience was awful with regards to those relationships...full of hurt and confusion, and deceit. Besides, I was on a mission to fulfill my intentions to create a fantastic life outside of Guyana, so I didn't allow the pain to linger.

Luckily, through my school years I managed to learn, and despite my environment and my shocking home life, I picked up vital information and many parts of my education stuck. Of course I wish more of it had stuck but I am delighted that ultimately, I learned the things that served me well in life. I am not a complete dummy and since I take full responsibility for dropping out of high school, I had to prove to myself that I have a decent brain. My friends and teachers were horrified that I was wasting my brain...in other words, not taking all the examinations necessary to proceed into university – the O Levels (GCSE) followed by A Levels, the British system.

Overall, my teenage years are somewhat of a blur. I see vivid sections of it when I was dealing with confusion and some seriously funny highlights with friends, parties, the stupidity of drinking and driving, and peer pressure. I definitely have blackout periods where it was unsavory, but there are victorious milestones, which I secretly celebrate with a smile and a self-embrace. There was simply no room in my teen years for academics, the luxury of studying and then going into university for another four years to learn more, only to think about a job after that and hopefully, earn money long into the future... I simply could not afford it.

My plan of action required me to put my hard-learned skillset into serving the goals I wanted immediately. I was seventeen years old and needed to use my life skills to get ahead of where I was and fast. I never considered failure. I always had my eyes on achieving the next step, and the next.

A Decade for Discovery

My sister moving to the British Virgin Islands was a turning point in her own life, and eventually, it became a pivotal point in mine too. She escaped a violent husband and started to enjoy life, albeit at the unimaginable price of losing her two sons (who chose to drink their father's Koolaid). She eventually found love, laughter, and happiness and I remember looking at my sister's face and feeling immense joy for her newfound freedom. I remember that day in Tortola and the warmth that washed over me. I remember marveling at how crazy life could be – just how much change is possible – and how grief and hurt could be overcome by the same magical ingredient in life: a loving partner.

I embraced everything that the BVI could offer. I sucked it up and learned. I stared at the shackles lying broken on the ground around me – the ones that had imprisoned me in Guyana, my childhood and teenage years. I put a most brave face on, and moved forward with my head held high. With my survival cloak tightly around me, lots of life lessons in my pocket, I lived a good life in Tortola.

My new job, nice people around me, new horizons with new things to learn, I felt very proud. I was never complacent and I was always learning and storing new information in multiple compartments. My brain is well exercised at running emotional marathons the past fifty years!

I reflect on my life in the BVI and compare it to surviving in Guyana. In one version, my head is mostly beneath the surface of the ocean, pushing up for breaths and gasping as I go under again; in the other, my head is out of the water. I could breathe and feel the sun on my face, but I was still kicking like mad to stay afloat and scared as hell. The emotions that I feel, particularly fear, I have learned to use well. It propels me to think and to create instead of feeling crippled by circumstance and complacency. The fleeting sensations that I have to curl up and lament or hide under a rock, I use it to replenish my energy, and to consider my options. That slow-mo picture of my life with too many scenes of me under a rock simply does not sit well.

My adult years were most welcomed and I continued to observe people in curious ways. I paid attention to whatever was happening around me – all of it shaped me – from my environment, to the strong and weak personalities around me, to bullies and uncompassionate lovers, some pretty horrific adults in my life just taking advantage, and my few opportunities to be vulnerable. It didn't crush me but made me stronger and gave me a tougher coat of armor, which I got used to wearing more often than not. My partners have all mentioned my armor at one point or another during our relationships. It intimidated them instead of stirring empathy.

I have to note that empathy is a learned skill and it takes a long, long time for some. My own adoption and demonstration of empathy has been a fifteen-year journey so far. I can appreciate that I have a long way to go and I look at my daughter and friends for inspiration and encouragement. I try to see them – really see them and what they are feeling, in order to drop my armour and allow raw feelings to soak in. Some days are harder than others to show that caring concern for others and I am working at it. Weird thing is I feel it; I can't always demonstrate it. My face is serious – that's my normal state. For me to smile, it takes conscious effort and frequent reminders.

While I didn't completely adopt the ways of the bullies that impacted my life early on, and I could have easily, it seems that my personality has formed by taking bits and pieces of different people in my life. I used to link all the strong, admirable qualities... Of course now that I am somewhat older (and questionably wiser) I know that I have created the necessary capabilities to get past bullying and use strong-armed tactics as and when I need to, and care and compassion at other times. There are definitely people in my life that would say I am too strong, too forceful at times, and with too little vulnerability and compassion. At the end of the day, it's what I have become and how I intend to live on this planet, how I continue to interact with people and make a positive impact before I die.

My Young Bold Professional Self

After a couple of frogs, I did find a prince charming – that's the way I saw him at the time. We were married two years later and had the most rewarding life together for another seven or eight years. It was an exciting life both professionally and personally for both of us, and it kept us happy and fulfilled. We explored Asia together and traveled the world. I put my smarts to great use and found jobs that propelled me onwards and upwards as my career years flew by. I was going in the right direction, learning, adapting, and putting all of that survival knowledge to excellent use. I loved my life because I kept expanding and challenging myself.

Throughout my twenties, I lived my life as if success was the only option. I didn't overthink what I was doing nor did I cite mantras or set aside time each day to practice mindfulness. I just lived my life with full intention to accomplish set goals, respect and engage with people around me, and enjoy my adventure. I am not an arrogant person, on the contrary. However, I considered my choices and made decisions guided by instinct and the hunger to be fulfilled.

I blossomed professionally, and I cruised intermittently, working smart and not as hard as some others I observed around me. I questioned my capabilities and ability to succeed in my field regularly; it was a constant exercise for me because I knew I was pushing, punching well above my weight. It kept me sharp and determined to get ahead of my competition. Whenever I felt I was slipping into second gear and it was becoming too easy, I would look for the next challenge – whether that was a job change, a tough client to pursue, a massive project that would expand me further, or something personally challenging to accomplish (like getting up Mount Kinabalu in Malaysia). Whenever I felt the need to be tested and stretched again, calling on my survival cloak to protect and even guide me in making hard decisions, I did it – for the stretch it provided.

After seven years of marriage, nine years of being together, my relationship with my husband became extremely dull and difficult. He wanted very different things compared to me. It became apparent that over the years of personal growth, he had gone down a very different path. Now eager to explore his intellect and puff up his academic feathers, he intended to turn his back on the life we had successfully built together; he wanted to become a student and pursue an intellectual path. I was, on the other hand, loving my career, personal growth, the respect I was earning from peers. I was in no way prepared to give it up to become the wife of a student. In my head, that meant making meals and cleaning floors and plumping cushions; I was not about to give up the incredible mental stimulation, which I was receiving everyday through my work. My career provided constant learning through the multicultural clients and diverse work projects in an exciting economic environment in Asia – it was addictive.

These crossroads also came at a time that we were just starting to try for a baby. Talk about bad timing. I suppose subconsciously the baby idea was meant to bind us together. We both wanted children but there is no doubt now that the timing led to a lot of the difficulties I had in getting pregnant. Repeated IVF treatments, pregnancies that survived six to eleven weeks, painful miscarriages, and ectopic pregnancies, all added to the massive rift that developed between us. We were incomprehensively sad, unhappy, and unable to provide solace and love or support for the other. In my lifetime, I pray never to see again two such sad souls making one couple.

I remember encouraging my husband at the time to write his thoughts down – to pen a book that could help other men in such a difficult position. Back in 1997, I don't recall seeing too much literature that shared other men's feelings around their partners' infertility and going through the pain of wanting to be a father and feeling so utterly helpless in dealing with sorrow. I felt pity and regret and sadness, but I could not help him. I had no empathy for him because I could not feel empathy or love for myself. My body would not cooperate in hosting our embryo and I was bitter and angry. Now, twenty-three years on I have some compassion for myself. I realize it was through no fault of mine and I have admitted that – but sometimes, just sometimes, that horrible voice in my head reminds me that it was my uterus that was uncooperative.

My life was full otherwise, as a young woman in my twenties – filled with exciting adventures and experiences through traveling and gorgeous friendships. I don't consider that I overcompensated for my infertility by overachieving in other areas of my life. I know that I went for it. Whatever I wanted to experience, I strived for it and worked towards it. I lived each week fully and deeply with emotion and passion.

My first job in Singapore was a result of me walking into an office, politely and assertively asking to speak with the boss, and engaging her in a conversation that would set me on a course of public relationships, communication, and customer service awareness for the rest of my life. When my young husband and I landed in Singapore with our suitcases and our small savings in our pockets, we dreamed big! We landed in that foreign city with a head full of hopes and two beaming faces. Not knowing anyone, we relied on resourcefulness and determination to push forward to carve out a life. And we did just that.

From the time I moved from Guyana to the British Virgin Islands, I spread my wings wide and I never looked back. To this day, I am deeply grateful for the international moves I've made and the places I've lived, and the people I've met and loved and enjoyed. As a young woman charging into the world, I felt empowered and enthusiastic and brave. I was truly capable and the world was my oyster and I lived that way. I was not a shrinking violet. I went after life and I lived voraciously.

My job search was strategic and focused from day one. I looked for firms that would benefit from having someone with my communication skill and presence, and I wrote what I thought to be compelling letters to each of them. I followed up diligently and even showed up in person at some of the firms so they could put a face to the resume. I was fearless and it was just this attribute that landed me my first role.

I am not ashamed to think of all the sinkholes I fell into. I know that I climbed out, muddy and dirty as hell, but I climbed out. Did I fall into other sinkholes? Hell yes, and sometimes, the same sinkhole seemed to beckon me even though I could recognize it a mile away. I learned hard lessons about me, about people, and about all the things that we experience living and sharing the planet with others. I've had incredible highs and lows with the loves in my life. All in all, the failures made me enjoy my victories even more.

At times, it was crushing to think that we humans have such a vile streak in us. We can be pretty cruel and calculating. But my survivor instinct took over in those incidents and I moved past without too many scars. There are a few deep emotional grooves but barely anything on the surface.

As a twenty-six-year-old, I remember feeling invincible. I was doing work that I loved, traveling around Asia, further afield for annual holidays, earning great money, meeting business leaders, and learning, and people were falling over themselves attracted to this vibrant young woman unafraid of living, in plain sight. I could see it on all their faces... I was infectious. My "smarts" were self-taught; I read everything I could get my hands on about the region, its business practices, cultural differences, and I researched the key people I would be meeting in corporate situations. I was armed with information and prepared for success.

At any age, this confidence can feed a whole life. It's remarkably powerful and the symbiotic relationships that blossom from one person projecting and exuding a healthy outlook full of promise and possibilities is infectious. At twenty-something I shared this gift, and now at fifty-something I have it. Yes, over various periods in my life, that bright spark was severely dimmed and I felt covered by soot, but I managed to look at those failures and accept they were only setbacks, temporary and necessary, in order to appreciate the full impact of my growth afterwards.

Surprisingly, I did not misuse my power with people. It never occurred to me that I could manipulate people and outcomes. My conscience was and still is quite pure. I am thankful every day that I am a good person. Besides, I didn't have to try and manipulate outcomes in my favor, because people were happy in my presence and I gave a positivity and optimism that was uplifting. I was successful as a result (if only professionally). My bosses loved me for my efficiency as much as for the impact I had on people around them.

I made friends – dear, wonderful, funny friends. Twenty-five years on they are still my friends – that must mean something! I have the best memories sitting in favorite restaurants in Singapore, Hong Kong, Bangkok, Bali, and other places around the world with my wonderful group of friends – laughing, talking, eating, and thinking,

"What else could there possibly be in life?" Those moments, those days and nights, are engraved in my heart and brain forever. It continues to be pure magic for me to have such a deep connection with people. Furthermore, I share those people and memories with my daughter. She has grown up surrounded by love and extended non-blood relatives who are "our village."

It was somewhere around twenty-four to twenty-six years old that I remember having a very big "Aha" moment... The deeper I connected with people emotionally, sincerely, the better our friendships and relationships grew. I looked into people's eyes. I noticed everything about them. I made it my mission to remember personal details so that I could ask them about it again when we met; I made an impact on how they felt. It showed because it made people even more attracted to me. I could see their eyes widening and their body go soft when I asked about an ailment, or their child, or something of interest to them they barely mentioned weeks ago. It made their world having someone acknowledge what was important in their lives. I noticed that about people early on.

Life took a somewhat downward spiral after my husband and I experienced the trauma of growing apart…a change in our paths when we grew professionally meant we had taken different turns. It became very hard to ignore, and combined with the pain and suffering of medical intervention to have a baby, life became quite dysfunctional and unbearable. We managed to hang on for another five years but it was brutal. How do people stay together and completely ignore their unhappiness? I simply cannot understand it. I wanted to end my marriage five years earlier than when it did end. I felt it in my gut. Instead, we lived in each other's shadow – ducking around each other at home, no conversation, no intimacy, and no joy.

My beautiful daughter, my champion, my shining light, and the person who inspires me most in this world to be genuine and live with purpose was a gift through adoption in Canada. We were chosen to be the parents of an amazing child – a file pulled out of hundreds of files sitting, waiting for a heavily pregnant young woman to choose us. Another memory that is emblazoned in my heart and brain forever is the moment when another human being handed their baby to me and said, "Take care of her." For a person to be so selfless is the highest honor someone could bestow on another, so special and unending. I have wondered several times in my life if I could ever give my baby to adoption if I had one... I still don't know if I am that big of a person. It is an astounding gift.

Peaks One and Two

I received two major gifts in my life in Vancouver, Canada, and I will eternally be grateful for both. It's the reason the city has a beautiful and special place in my life. The first was pursuing therapy and counseling for the very first time. After the hurt of losing many pregnancies and knowing that I would do whatever it took to have a child in my life, I decided I needed to understand what type of parent I might be and, to a large degree, deal with a lot of unresolved issues I had with my parents and my upbringing. By this time, I considered myself very lucky to have come out the other side and be relatively sane. I had left Guyana and all its shackles behind, built my life up successfully over the years with jobs I loved, experiences in traveling and making wonderful friends who were loyal and remarkable in ways I never knew possible, and I was secure in a comfortable material existence. But there was a heavy stone that rested inside my chest. I felt it regularly.

Counseling was a godsend to me and I learned a lot about myself. I was finally able to understand and accept a lot about me. I blamed myself less and I started to understand the negative impact that my parents had on me. My work was now cut out and I had to undo quite a bit to allow more positive thinking and habits to develop. I had to learn to let go of that dark period that was not a childhood. It would be a hard journey…learning to let go.

The most profound gift in Vancouver was our daughter. The decision to pursue adoption was easy for us and thankfully, my husband accepted that we could not have a biological child. We were incredibly lucky and our baby came to us a year after we completed our file and background checks and placed our dossier with an agency. The magical illusion became reality and Maya Sugar was born in September 1999. The hurt, sadness, and everything black melted away when she was put into my arms. I knew in that instant that I would not let this human being down and that I would protect her with my life should it be necessary.

Soon after our daughter was given to us, we accepted that we no longer cared much for each other. Our attention was focused only on her and I made the decision to move on, rather than remain in a loveless marriage. I doubt my ex-husband will ever forgive me for making that decision. It blew our worlds up and made my daughter extremely unhappy because she was unable to see her dad every day. For twelve years, I beat myself up badly thinking that I should not have put my daughter through a divorce. I have made myself wretched and desperate as I berate my soul for putting my own happiness above that of my child's. It's been one heck of a journey to get to this place of acceptance. Now I acknowledge that it was absolutely necessary for me to find my happiness in order to be a good parent.

Prior to my daughter's arrival, I questioned parenthood – my own parents who shook my core in a bad way – both parents frightful and unprepared for the role they ignored. I questioned, how I would be as a parent? Which virtues and faults would I present to my child? And any promises that I made to her, how would I fare in keeping them?

The process for putting together our file for adoption involved a great deal of digging into our lives by the agency and social worker. Some of those interviews unearthed thoughts and discussions that we hadn't dreamed of or considered before. It was unsettling to say the least and it continued my own personal growth in a bizarre way. Coupled with therapy, it gave me priceless insight and I sat for hours mulling over the details, which I found fascinating about myself and how my mind works.

I am not a typical daydreamer but I started to journal in earnest. My scribbles filled volumes of notebooks in a year and I piled them all on my bedside table.

Once we passed the various psychological tests, we had a sparkling dossier prepared and put on display for all birth parents to ponder. It was nerve-wracking but in the end, and not after a long wait, we had the most amazing call.

The little baby girl bestowed upon us by her birth mother turned out to be the most positive and sensitive soul in my life to date. She has the raw vulnerability and consciousness that I admire and envy. Yet, I see her competitiveness and determination and I know she will be fantastic in creating her place in this world. The discussion around nature versus nurture occupied our conversations for many months when our daughter was a toddler... I can see the evidence now of course, just how powerful nurture is and how it can complement or deter a person's natural instinct. I hope each and every year that goes by, that I've managed to keep my daughter's shining light alive and healthy despite my down days. I have the utmost respect for her powerful sense of self and capacity to be vulnerable and sensitive. She's old enough now to tell me that I have not been a bad influence.

As a result of my own experience, I feel adoption is a sacred oath. When people choose to adopt a baby, they make a commitment for life to be the best parents possible, not at the detriment or over burden of one's self, but certainly to push hard beyond one's limitations and comfort to be the best they could be for that child – that sacred gift.

I knew early on during my daughter's toddler years that I would be the best person I could be as a result of her existence. She will be the legacy that I leave on this planet, a dynamic woman who shows her love for life and to make a positive impact on people. So much dwells inside her already. My role, I recognize early, is simply to guide her virtues and morality and acceptance of diversity. I have lived every year knowing and staying on course with that commitment. Each year, my daughter surprises me with how much she has grown emotionally and spiritually. As an eighteen-year-old, during the time I am writing these words, she is my inspiration to continue to be real and brave.

Loving Yourself Can Be Painful to Others

People go through divorce, heartache, depression, and horrendous self-doubt. I know this firsthand. I also know that there is a fierce unexplainable bond between a mother and her child that exists, and during stressful times, that bond can warm and bind even stronger, sometimes to the complete exclusion of others.

I have beaten myself up many, many times for putting my daughter through my splits, me moving homes, and the terrible disruption to our lives. However, I know that I am a far better woman and mother for moving away from loveless places filled with discontent. Should I have stayed in unhealthy and unfulfilling relationships, my daughter would not have had great parenting from me. I try to explain it each year, with more sophisticated and age-appropriate language, as she gets older. It's one of my deep-seated sources of guilt but I would not change a thing in a "do-over."

My genuine fear is that a child of divorce or multiple splits could feel that relationships are disposable and that if people do not fit together any more, we move on. I know just how hard I worked to even the bumps and stay committed in my relationships. I have spent time explaining to her the difference between simply moving on, and staying true to what I felt I needed in my life to be content and happy. To an outsider it could well appear that's what I have done in my past, but in my heart I know that's not what I did; I tried really hard.

When a woman stops feeling loved and intimate with the man lying in bed beside her, does she have to stay and bottle her inner, deeper feelings? Have I in my lifetime overrated intimacy, passion, hot-as-hell and wobbly knees lust? You see, I don't think so. Every person, not just women, should feel that emotion pumping through them regularly to feel alive and pulsating and wanted, in a raw sense. I firmly believe that great physical chemistry is as vital as air, water, and food.

We are human beings and we are hard-wired to feel. Otherwise, we are dull and numb and become zombies reacting to things. How on earth do people live passionate lives till they are in their early or mid-thirties, then slip into mind-numbing uneventful, flat-line existence? Where is their self-value, their personal fulfillment, or their pulse? I have seen in my lifetime, far too many women who have children, then hang up their sense of humor and their sex drive and deep-seated needs. It's downright insane and I akin it to a ticking time bomb just waiting… How can smart grown-ups do that to themselves and then say, "It's for the children's sake."

Although I have not been one to take up various trends in relationship management, like date night, or couple time, I have practiced logic and reason. The baby came second after my husband; so naturally, I made sure I had time for him. Baby went to bed by 7 pm, which gave us lots of time for evenings together; we went out for meals and left her with a reliable babysitter guilt-free. Later on, when she was around five or six years old, she went on sleepovers as long as I investigated and felt secure that the families were safe and clean. There wasn't any worry on the child to frighten her about sleeping outside of home. I encouraged it and I reciprocated as much as possible for my child's social skills to develop.

I have seen many parents who limit themselves and their children by their irrational beliefs and glass ceilings. It's uncanny how this still happens today. Whenever I heard friends or other women talk about what they don't do, or won't have their child do, it screams LIMITS to me. Of course, I appreciate there are specific circumstances when none of this applies. But for the most part, I believe parents and adults, and in many cases, women, put too many limitations on themselves and their loved ones... This stifles a real chance to be fulfilled and for them to be excited with living. I am not referring to things that cost money – I am referring to a mindset.

It's only in my forties that I seriously started to unpack the monkeys on my back…removing them one by painful one. Even though I spent so many years early on gauging and learning about people and considering their actions and behaviors, I still managed to pile on a few heavy gorillas over the decades. I am seriously pleased now that I am over the half-century mark, I feel more empowered and alive than my first three decades. Once in a while, a sneaky monkey will climb right back on but I am being extra careful to recognize them coming my way.

A major turning point in my life making brave and hard decisions was after my first divorce – it took every bit of mental strength and my survival learning to come through and look after my two-and-a-half-year-old alone. Not unscathed but with sufficient energy and focus to keep putting one foot in front the other, I lived in a sterilized bubble during our separation and divorce. I drew heavily on my survival skills and was hyper-aware of my circumstances and my would-be predators. Although a very scary time in my life, I considered my decision carefully, and the reality that would follow. The way for me to prepare for my circumstances was to face them full on – kinda like driving a car... You have to keep looking ahead and all around you simultaneously, so you're not surprised by the stop sign or the pedestrian or cyclist. Eventualities and the unforeseen are as certain as well-made plans.

Playing with a Very Hot Flame

I was extremely careful not to get involved in anything that could affect my baby, but I was out there and walking a tight rope. I explored new things and dug deep to uncover my most inner desires and the things I wanted in life. An important boundary that was questioned was my sexual appetite. My newly found liberation set me free on many levels – horribly cliché but very true.

Unfortunately, the lifestyle aspects could only titillate me for so many hours of the day. I had to face my reality that I had a future taking care of my little one and common sense kept my feet on the ground. I am very grateful for my ability to see things sensibly in the end – it has kept me from self-destructing. Survival instinct fueled my entrepreneurialism, and when I considered what I had to do to earn a living and provide food and shelter, I made hard choices and went into business leveraging my talents, skillset, and network. Although finding a job would have been easier, I decided to start my own consulting firm so that I could spend quality and quantity time with my daughter through her toddler years.

During this period of immense transition, I made new friendships and enjoyed a whole new lifestyle. It was addictive and pleasing, and I am delighted that it energized me to be a happier person. Being a suppressed and lonely wife used to make my days as a loving mother extremely difficult. However, having these other sides open up in my life gave me wings and a sunny outlook to be more fulfilled and content.

Overall, I felt like a whole person – big chunks which had been missing were now filled in like vital, colorful putty. Actually, I felt a little bit like that invincible young woman who soared in Tortola, BVI. I realized I hadn't felt like that for many years because I had been busy dealing with punches and swings from growing up and being a parent and a partner and acting responsibly.

Through my twenties and thirties I had dipped in and out of pursuing what was meaningful to me. Simultaneously, I had gotten very busy with life. My husband, my pursuit of career opportunities and professional growth, my daughter, being a great friend, and enjoying the material spoils of an international lifestyle, I had been wandering on and off the path very happily. However, I was mostly guided by what was right and responsible as far as others were concerned. I did not truly focus on what I wanted, or how I wanted to live my life. Giving happiness to others was more important.

I could never regret my life as I lived it during those glorious decades. I worked hard and played larger. No regrets! But I wasn't fully my authentic self through my first three-and-a-half decades… I was lying dormant and ignoring some very important cues.

As part of my liberation, I also lost a great love. My partner and I went our separate ways after he smashed my heart into a million pieces. I crumbled, and recovery from this loss took a long while. For the first time ever, I felt genuinely crushed with heartache. It was and still is, the most pain I have ever felt from losing someone. At the time of our breakup, I saw his act only as selfish. Now, I ponder on his right to be happy and content and he obviously wasn't with me, so he moved on. When I decided to be true to my feelings and live accordingly, it was only natural to expect that others would reciprocate and they would make decisions that would be out of my control. The partner I loved and cherished no longer felt the same love with me. It was a slap in the face for sure, but one I had to accept. My ego was crushed.

Friendship poured in from the most unexpected places and I felt closer to people than I had for years. I had not expected that reaction from his friends and I was deeply moved. I look back, and I embrace and treasure these people and their love and support. Immediately after the breakup, I think I was deadened by grief and being overwhelmed, I didn't express my gratitude sufficiently. I've made up for that now and I tell my friends consistently how much I value and love them. I knew then that I had a powerful village around me and it was truly uplifting.

After many months of grief, sadness, and sobbing, I lifted my head, felt the ache in my heart, and moved on. I started over with a new home, a place for my darling daughter, and a new job. I landed on my feet with a great deal of poise and integrity. I had survived a painful blow and came away licking my wounds but feeling proud of me. Frankly, it still hurt like hell some days, but I don't think too much about the hurt. I focus on why I had to survive and thrive. My life and my daughter's life are more important than licking wounds and hoping for the best. I had been hurt emotionally, but I walked away sexually liberated and understanding new facets to my personality. These revelations gave me a new lease on self-confidence and worth.

My recharged vigor extended to my work situation as well. I had been developing and growing multiple communication agencies the past five years and successfully making their owners healthy margins while delivering outstanding work for clients. It was at this juncture that I walked away from a very comfortable paycheck, to put my own name above the front door and on the letterhead. My uncomfortable decision to strike out on my own and set up my own communication firm was made considerably more palatable when three loyal clients confirmed they would move their business to my agency immediately. It was like getting an injection of testosterone, dopamine, adrenaline, AND oxytocin. I floated up to a cloud and stayed there for some time.

In business and in my personal life, I feel the fire in my belly. I started my agency with one fabulous employee who also followed me from another firm and grew my business five-fold in its first year. I had multiple clients from various industry sectors, and I was the intrepid entrepreneur and salary provider for three very committed and talented people after one year. My agency produced creative and highly effective communication solutions for clients and our reputation grew in a market that was saturated with homegrown and international agencies vying for the same clients' budgets.

I continued to hone a successful strategy for my firm's sustainability and growth, and I positively thrived and blossomed. Clients were bigger, international brands across a wide range of industries, and I created 'sweet spots' for our work, so we shone brightly in special areas when pursuing new pitches and niche projects. All in all, the risk to compete with established service providers and become a well-regarded agency when pitching for Singapore government contracts paid off extremely well, in terms of utter satisfaction and pride.

The fact is I never overthink these decisions. It came from the necessity for me to get out of a deep rut; I did everything that felt logical and natural to build a successful business and employ great people while delivering the quality of work I expected from myself. It was intuitive for me to just get on with it. Consider my options, hone in on a decision, make a plan, (no plan B), get to it, and keep adjusting as necessary to succeed: that's my modus operandi.

Choose the People Around You

From early on in my work life, I recognized that I am a highly collaborative person. I share ideas and I like to invite discussion and dissection. I enjoy seeing ideas stretched, passed, annihilated, and reconfigured. For me, that's the true meaning of creativity. When something is solo germinated, it's lacking color and flavor, instead of an idea that is shared and considered by many perspectives. This streak enabled me to motivate and build the team within my firm as well as develop excellent partnerships over time.

My staff co-created a culture of cohesion and creativity with a lot of intelligence and fun. I could not have scripted it any better. It was a young entrepreneur's ultimate dream. As our client list grew, so did our specialisms and our reputation with it. Till now, I know and appreciate the people who worked for and with me, and I am eternally grateful for their loyalty, commitment, and hard work. It warms my heart when I see them and we share a meal, which is rare but still possible.

The name for my agency was born at a glorious dinner table one night with dear friends over lychee martinis and a plethora of delicious Malaysian food. Well into the evening, stuffed to the gills, we started to discuss what an agency name should reflect...my friends knowing that this was of huge importance to me – the entire undertaking of opening my own, discussed the merits of something self-indulgent and resonant. I think a tiny bit vain too...why not? I was embarking on a great adventure in more ways than one. Siren-Communication was incorporated, complete with a fabulous red logo, and a very proud Founder & Managing Director proceeded to get business cards printed.

In addition to feeling immensely satisfied, I believe it was one of the first times that I truly sat back and allowed myself a well-deserved "pat on the back." I had rarely done this in the past; one goal achieved, another one set – this used to be my pattern. However, looking at my company ID, printing my cards, walking into that tiny yet impressive serviced office in the financial center, Shenton Way in Singapore, I felt my heart swell and I was bursting with self-confidence and happiness. This must be what it feels like to skydive!

I often stopped what I was doing at my laptop to look out the window, look around our office and my first employee, and submit to the fright and excitement that flooded my brain and body. The fright was a good indicator for me to appreciate that I was challenging myself and growing in ways necessary to make my business a success. I told myself over and over that my employee was relying on me for a salary and I could not fail as a result. It worked. Again, with instinct and logic as my trusted companions, I was masterful at seeking out new business, meeting potential clients, presenting well-composed and thoughtful ideas, and most of all, connecting with people with whom I would collaborate and share expertise.

Till today, this is a skill and a highly tuned attribute that I admire in people. It is the not-so-secret ingredient to successful entrepreneurship and business development. I found collaboration to be highly rewarding and I am going back at least eighteen years, in Southeast Asia, where the culture in business mainly promoted holding your cards very close to your chest so that no one could steal your ideas! I bucked that trend and pioneered with my staff and my clients, a way of exploring seed ideas to evolve and grow the best ones. This sharing had its pitfalls but mostly, it generated great results in terms of well thought-out solutions and garnered significant respect from partners who worked with us.

When it came to contract negotiations and fees, I treated that the same way. Businesses i.e. people, get into a provider/customer arrangement to exchange a product or service for a fee. Both parties must walk away with a certain amount of satisfaction in order to consider that transaction a successful one. I have in my career spent too many hours with procurement people who felt it necessary to pummel their contractors down to the last $100, in order to feel like they had done their jobs. I used to sit back and watch their faces twitch and their pens making hasty scribbles as they calculated and recalculated numbers. In the end, my honesty with them either secured the deal, or I walked away to avoid feeling like I had been raped and plundered. I set up my business to deliver great work and to make a profit. Choosing to be in business with honorable people is a conscious decision one can make.

Till now, I ask myself who do I like spending time with, being around and engaging in conversation. I seek out positive people who generally have an unapologetic approach to life; they handle good and bad, all in stride as part of living.

Pick the three or four people in your life, who live relatively close-by for face-to-face interactions, with whom you truly enjoy being, and spend quality time. It feeds our soul to have such connections and to allow ourselves to be. There is no façade, no preparations, simply exhaling in the moment and genuinely expressing who we are. It's utterly symbiotic too. It's easy to see and to feel the energy and vibrancy that is shared between strangers who become friends or trusted colleagues.

We are human and we are beings. Both those definitions require others for us to live – feel, learn, and express ourselves openly. It's a formula for rejuvenation that is deeply rewarding and, in my mind, should be enjoyed and shared regularly.

Successful Entrepreneurship Takes Courage

As I meet more unhappy and dissatisfied career professionals, they seem to be leaning towards starting their own businesses as a "knee-jerk" reaction to their situations. To many, being an entrepreneur means being in control of their time…a popular misunderstanding. When I talk about being a successful entrepreneur versus being an entrepreneur, eyebrows raise and with some, there is the silent acknowledgment "yes, of course."

Having a vision, an idea for a business is the easiest part. Building it successfully to develop a customer base, getting the news out in the market that you exist, and realizing consistent sales and profitability takes considerable maneuvering and effort. A fluid strategy, real time market and consumer research to understand the environment, and effective communication are all vital ingredients. Add to this your ability to use common sense in order to consider various other factors – competitors' activities, timing and relevance, and the nuts and bolts of operating your business, and you'll find that your days are filled and even consumed, with the delights of building something that is yours.

That is indeed the sweetening which many new entrepreneurs lose sight of. It's not so much you in control of your time; it's the fact that you are investing energy and grit into something that will reward you one hundred percent. You are in control of how it grows and how much profit you take. The criteria to make important decisions are wholly yours and if it doesn't sit well, then you bin that decision and go back to the drawing board. Being a successful business owner draws on your ability to be honest about what you can do and how much external help you should seek.

My business mentorship and coaching is specifically aimed at owners who have launched their ideas, have been skipping along, not particularly growing, and perhaps, even on the verge of slipping off the hillside. The idea for a business may remain relevant and viable; however, market conditions and consumer habits change continuously. Therein lies the need to have a dynamic strategy and a fresh look at who and how you're engaging with customers. Business owners spend a lot of time excited to launch and then run on adrenaline to keep things developing the first year or two; however, marketing becomes a conflict with profit, and whatever creative or operational talent is lacking in pushing that business further faster is blissfully ignored.

A common pattern I've also encountered is one where founders refuse to hire someone more suitable for the business to manage it profitably, and to make hiring decisions. Some entrepreneurs are great at the setup but they are not good when it comes to making money, or building and motivating the right team for growth.

Becoming an entrepreneur means there is an element of risk-taking…and something is to be provided in return for a profit, if not monetary then of some value to the owner. It should also be considered that the original idea may well evolve quickly to something else and successful entrepreneurs understand and embrace this. Creativity and innovation can come from necessity, such as when there is a "do-or-die" situation, or it can grow from sound research and a visionary person leading the charge. Often, when an entrepreneur opens up their vision to shared talents, it means you're getting the benefit of their lessons from their own failures and successes; the business plan becomes a well-crafted music sheet with each chord and timing almost perfectly balanced.

I used to think it was an Asian trait to hold your cards extremely close to your chest and saying very little in business meetings, shaking heads one way when in fact, the opposite was being communicated. Now of course, I recognize it to be a global trait amongst certain types of business people. They cannot share their thoughts or ideas openly for fear of someone stealing from them. I witness this in many business owners who would otherwise benefit significantly, if they were to adopt a different perspective. Right here in Vancouver, too many experienced entrepreneurs continue to hang onto their original vision and business plan with white knuckles, complaining that: "Things are tough. It's hard." Yet, intuitively they understand the value of collaboration and what it could do for their companies.

In markets where consumers are from diverse cultural backgrounds, i.e. an immigrant population, isn't it smart to integrate diversity and make it work for your marketing so that you leverage a variety of ideas to reach that catchment?

Without a calculated risk to embrace and leverage other ways of thinking and complimentary talent into a vision we hold, businesses run a high chance of barely surviving, if at all, in today's highly dynamic environment. On the flipside, I see the way in which some entrepreneurs, especially women, reach out on Facebook pages to seek advice, support each other, and share their thoughts (sometimes incessantly). Despite the plethora of questions and answers, after what could only be described as a flurry of activity for a day or two, they disappear and I wonder if they made any significant adjustments to their plans. Barely a few days later, other entrepreneurs will ask similar questions on those pages...

Achieving success in running your own business takes guts! There is no reward in being brave some days, cowering from hard truths on others, and ignoring your own weaknesses. In a marketplace where consumers are multicultural, our thinking has to match.

Perfection Is Painful

There have been many times in my life that I yearned for the ideal – in love, on holidays, food, and in the work I did. I enjoyed what I felt to be perfection on many occasions, but getting to the realization that the journey there was, too fraught with nerves, enabled me to learn and appreciate a new perspective. Perfection could be the small cherry on my cake but really, the big tasty cake is where I should spend more time dining with enjoyment.

Too many seek perfect conditions to pursue something. The ability to take risks and adjust one's course in midstream seems to have diminished over the past two decades. More time is spent considering and zigzagging over hypothetical plans, and far too little time is spent using logic and common sense to guide people to get on with their lives and what they want to do in it.

I fully appreciate that people consider more is at risk these days – but is it? My young husband and I had lots at risk when we gave up our lives in the British Virgin Islands to travel across the world, land in Singapore with some cash and our clothes, to pound the pavement, and look for work. If we had failed and spent all of our savings, we would have had a very different history. However, we got on with our plans to find work and make a life there. We planned, changed, and adapted as necessary, and simply didn't let "bad days" get us down. Yes, there were bad days receiving many rejection emails on our applications, or handling curt, dismissive phone calls, but we pushed on. We dealt with discouragement by joining the YMCA and swimming hard laps or smashing a squash ball.

Learning to work with colleagues in Asia was a massive undertaking – cultural differences, communication nuances, the importance of hierarchy, and other traditional influences, all added up to challenges which stretched me further. I didn't lament the hard work and effort; I welcomed the adventure and the tools it gave me. I took it upon myself to bring my global outlook and marry it with cultural norms to create a work ethic that would fit my new environment. It paid off splendidly because it resonated with locals in the region who saw the added value I brought in my approach to business and people skills.

Along with other monkeys, the "perfection gorilla" sometimes tries to climb onto my back and I frequently dodge it now. It's mostly in the way I expect a great deal from myself, and in turn, I subconsciously set the bar higher for people around me. It's not sustainable and it's far better to accept reality, to change and adapt as I go along, acknowledging there are unexpected surprises flavoring the journey. This is not to say I do not stick to my goals; once I have an intention set, you'd be hard-pressed to find someone more determined and driven. All I am pointing out is that we can do much better when we accept changes and challenges and deal with them in stride. Take it all in, and point your way strategically and fluidly to the goal posts.

To be fair, I've been able to practice this more easily in business than in my personal life. I find myself expecting my love life to be amazing. From time to time, I ask myself why not! It should be fantastic. However, since one's love life includes another person, it goes without saying that such pressure on a poor unsuspecting soul could have consequences and be fraught with misunderstandings. An acceptance of differences inherently means perfection is defined in an assortment of ways – tiers of perfection perhaps, instead of a single bull's eye.

My first husband accused me of being an idealist when it came to relationship and marriage. I spent quite a number of years questioning his statement. While I fully accept diversity in people and their ways of thinking and doing, I know that I will always hold love and companionship in the highest regard and that I want from my partner, something deeply special and intimate that makes its mark on both our souls for whatever period of time we choose to spend together. That doesn't sound like the definition of idealist to me.

In my work as a coach, I speak with many young professionals and intelligent university students who are ambitious and striving for greatness. Whether their goals are subconscious or intentional, they stress themselves in the most illogical ways because they avoid facing their own hard truths. Goals and achievements seem to be benchmarked with what's current, instead of what's right for each of them, and to some degree, what's possible –

given their capabilities. I am not suggesting that people should aim lower and avoid reaching for their dreams; I am recommending that regular self-checks with reality and what you're genuinely passionate about and capable of will get you far closer to your dreams. Having unrealistic expectations equates to banging your head against concrete walls and it leaves you with severe concussion, pain, and regret.

If dreams were easy to reach, they wouldn't by definition be called "dreams." But working hard for your dreams, armed with more than enthusiasm and hope, gives you a far better chance of securing them.

Humility, Ego, and Vanity – Check!

I have been likened to a man on various occasions – in the boardroom, and in matters of the heart. I suppose it's a mix of nature and nurture, as well as who and what I've become with experience.

Being in business and carving out the opportunities I have with people across international firms, traveling and soaking up the elements of foreign culture, and being open to the challenges and lessons which each situation presented have all stroked and spanked my ego differently. If you've ever felt like you had the proverbial "slap on the face," or a bucket of cold water poured over your head, be sure to take the time and courage to learn from that lesson. I have been raked over hot coals on several occasions – extremely humbling and utterly painful.

I embarrass easily and that is why I am properly prepared when I enter a room. I take few risks when it comes to ignorance and that's only when it's virtually impossible to further my own education. My ego, larger in my twenties and thirties, has had enough attention to bring it to a size that serves me well now. I value my ego; it helps me to strive for better and to ditch complacency when I might be tempted. There are many conversations taking place around leaving our ego at the door when we enter into a relationship – professionally or otherwise. I understand the arguments however. I would apply that having a purposeful ego could in fact become one of our greatest champions in pushing our achievements further.

Humility on the other hand is a work in progress throughout our lives, and with each phase, we go higher or lower on the scale. It's not hard to be humble, but it's hard to be humble all the time when we are outperforming our competitors, or when we are extremely proud due to a milestone achievement. Shouldn't we allow some measure of arrogance to feed us once in a while? If humility can keep us on the "straight and narrow," and out of harm's way when working closely with other people, wouldn't a purposeful ego help propel our aspirations further and establish our position on the leader board? Isn't this the whole point when we compete in business, exams, bid for something we want? The saying that "it's all about the journey" surely is true only half the time. What about winning? There is something interesting and deeply satisfying about getting there first for a reason.

People who have known me for more than half my life will use "modest" and "arrogant" in describing me at different times. I've struck a balance and I know well enough what's bubbling inside and what's spilling out when it comes to my emotions. Humility for me is absolutely critical in my everyday life. I embrace every aspect of it when I leave my house and walk into society. I receive the brightest smiles, the kindest gestures, and the most unexpected responses when I am giving humility.

When it comes to breaking barriers and engaging with people from all different backgrounds, humility is one of the most precious attributes one can possess.

I consider myself meticulous when it comes to my appearance and I am, for the most part, quite a vain person. From a very young age, I remember taking good care of myself – as a child, I loved my brand new uniforms for the start of a school term. I was particular about my hair and the shade of black ribbons that tied my braids, which by the way had to be symmetrical and straight on each side of my head (much to the chagrin of my mother); my nails were kept short and clean. I didn't have to be encouraged to be particular about these things. I just was! In my teen years, I remember commenting on my girlfriends' appearance. I thought they tried to paint on different features rather than accentuate the beautiful ones they had. Weirdly, I hate looking into a mirror or any reflective surface and to this day, I can get dressed without one, except to apply mascara, and I leave the house without so much as an approval check.

As far as fitness and good health are concerned, I work hard to stay in shape throughout my adult years. I love feeling healthy, and whenever severely stressed, I turn to exercise and sports to blast out the negative emotions. Throughout my career as a corporate communication consultant, I dressed as you might expect a chic, sophisticated managing director of a top professional firm would – even when I was the junior executive! My bosses over time commented on this and I was a great ambassador for whichever brand I carried on my business card. This extended naturally to when I owned my agency; I cultivated a culture of style and when "casual Fridays" became a thing I cringed and it took some time for me to agree a happy medium with my own staff.

I firmly believe there is an unconscious bias that takes place in our society, and particularly the workplace when it comes to appearance. If you groom and dress well, chances are much higher you will command a greater level of engagement and interaction. This experiment plays out in our daily lives and there is a lot to be said for "dress for success." Empowerment is possible through the way we present ourselves in private and public, and our emotional and mental states can become heightened and happier as a result of the impact we see on people's faces.

Consider how you feel after a long enjoyable walk or a delicious well-balanced meal? How powerfully you stare in the mirror when you try on beautiful clothes? Or, your reaction when someone pays you a fantastic compliment… Could you consciously use vanity, humility, and your ego to provide clues as to what's working and what isn't? Like so many things in life, it's getting the balance right, isn't it?

Awareness = Admission of Talent and Shortcoming

No doubt, easier said than done – to admit to one's inabilities as easily as one's talents and assets cannot be natural for many. We can identify with our strengths and experience but when it comes to facing what we cannot think and do is much, much harder. Just as collaboration with others does not come easily for some!

Consequently, there is less truth amongst us as human beings and admitting our genuine selves to partners in life and business can be a real struggle. We are, in many ways, peacocks. What if we played instead, as ordinary and beautiful brown hens? What if our innate beauty and capacity came shining through without much titivating or too much language? What if we continued to play without self-impressed rules – just as children do for a while, and even they begin to impress rules on each other past a certain age!

The chemistry between people fascinates me – what we do as employers and employees, man and woman, parent and child. In professional relationships, I believe there is a great need for people to admit to their inability to do certain things. Starting with management, human resourcing departments, and down to the candidates who seek to be part of an organization – when we admit to having a passion for certain things, a natural ability in other areas, a learned way to execute responsibilities, balanced with the lack of understanding and a void in specific capabilities, it would help so much in avoiding miscommunication and misrepresented or misplaced authority. Clarity and honesty is a much-needed commodity when presenting ourselves to the external world. I believe it would lessen the burden on our own self if we could find such honesty.

This lends itself to diversity in people and how we accept each other. The way in which we view people from around the world as they enter our communities can be with a less competitive lens and more with "how do they complement me and what I can do." If you are a social entrepreneur, you can embrace the concept that integrating foreign talent into your business or professional service can provide people with a wealth of opportunities for mutual benefit. In the "for profit" sector, too little common sense is being exercised to take advantage of each other's failures and successes.

Competition is supremely important, and integration of diversity is a critical development in our global outlook to maintain a competitive edge. How we speak and engage with new people (immigrants) at our supermarkets, libraries, petrol stations, and at our children's schools will create a dynamic shift in the growth and cultural development of communities. Right down to the words we choose, this will make a massive difference in the way we engage.

In an ideal world, meritocracy would rule and the best person for the situation would get it. However, so many other factors play a part now and the ever grown importance of contacts and connections far outweigh skill, to the detriment of best outcome. Comfort and security does not allow for people to take risks on others who are outside their familiar zone. I see too many risk averse decisions taken on a daily basis – personally and professionally by very smart people.

While I see a very important role for companies and their human resources departments to reformulate the way in which we interview foreigners, I believe people speaking to each other differently at the ground level will change those interview questions over a shorter period of time. We will be able to smile at the differences and embrace the skillset and passion that we do not have ourselves yet admire, and be able take those language nuances and kindness into the boardroom.

As I coach business owners, I see the struggle they have trying to do it all themselves. Considering that most communities have been impacted in some way by globalization and immigration, wouldn't it make sense to bring onboard some different talents outside our own, in order to keep businesses competitive and relevant? There are significant fears – how do we address them rationally to make more small and medium-sized businesses sustainable and profitable?

Admission of the lack of a specific skillset will help to attract talent who can complement a founder's vision. My philosophy in looking at any business that is selling something – customers are people with ever changing appetites and moods; it takes more than one brain to effectively stay ahead of demand and try to be ready for where they'll land next (the customers). That fabulous and famous analogy: "Be where the (ice hockey) puck will be" by Wayne Gretzsky to be successful in scoring.

One of my frustrations with relationships is the fact that in the beginning, people tend to portray only their best selves – man, woman, seeking to impress – saying nice things, looking their best, and making significant efforts to hide any flaws. Somehow, we seem unable to be ourselves and allow the other person to have a look at who we are naturally. I know we have a biological reason for this and we follow what our brain propels us to do. However, in so many ways, we have evolved and we know that being ourselves is really the only way to attract someone who will stick around. If we could get to know each other without facades right from the first meeting, wouldn't that be far more meaningful and worthwhile? Is anyone seeking perfection these days?

The three long-term partners in my life have all been drastically different people – absolutely nothing in common, except that they have been men. With each partner, I refreshed myself at the start with who I was and the characteristics that define me. Seemed to be the right thing to do to remind myself that I have a strong will and that I should allow them to see the person I am on the inside. I take goals and achievements quite seriously, and I continuously strive for active living. I am not a dormant person by any stretch and some people find that tiresome after the honeymoon period.

The Potholes Are in Plain Sight

The over-riding emotion that has filled me (mostly) throughout the past fifty years is not one I am proud of. I wish it was love, laughter, happiness, and joy; I could accept all those peppered with the other less feel-good emotions like hurt, disappointment, sadness, and loss. But survival has been my close partner, guide, and cloak since I was a child. Survival has driven me and it has protected me. It made me stronger but also, it prevented me from doing things that might have had a nicer outcome. Survival has been a bittersweet tonic so far and now, I must look very hard to redesign my relationship with it.

After a glorious period of being alone, basking in my independence, my success in starting a new firm, and having a beautiful and happy home for my daughter, I gambled on a new relationship with a man.

Of course hindsight being what it is, I could ask for a "do-over." I ignored very important cues and dismissed my instinct. Stupid, stupid, stupid!!! We both thought that a second marriage ought to be sensible, with considered risk and maturity that comes with being in your late forties. Well, think again. Matters of the heart make us the stupidest creatures on this planet.

The people in my life recognize this about me; I am on the go doing interesting things whenever I can. I love to learn, I love to experience things, and I think about things. In order to avoid making the same mistakes again and again (or so I believe), I reflect regularly on my thoughts and actions. I have a large box full of journals, which I have written diligently whenever I was going through mega crap in my life. Writing for me is soothing and therapeutic, and reading my journals during good times gives me fantastic insight into myself.

Whenever I fell hard, I reflected and made lists of what works and what doesn't – how I was feeling and why, what brought the gorilla onto my back, and how I was going to crawl out from under the hairy beast. Each time I succeeded in getting out of a deep pothole, I patted myself on the back and assured myself that I was worth the hard work and the big dreams. Lucky for me, I have the work ethic and deep-seated hunger to succeed from my immigrant parents. Failures and successes in my life are like lessons taught by a master teacher – in my head, Mother Nature was slapping me in the face hard – with good reason and with good result. However, true to being a human, I have repeated some mistakes, albeit differently.

The toughest challenges for me have been in relationships; I am told I'm a great friend and a wonderful wife. But somehow, over time and with repetition, my ability to balance my own needs and stay true to who I am gets diminished and I focus too much on making my partner's life easy and pleasurable. The cycle of making myself exhausted doing things for someone else then kicks into high gear and I start to annoy myself and feel resentment. Of course, my partners were never to blame for this recurring habit of mine. It was all me. And the kicker is I am not a people-pleaser at all. I never could be…except in these relationships with the men in my life where I gave too much and simply did not give myself the permission to take anything away for me.

Another recurring pothole for me has been to bite my tongue and avoid saying what I truly felt immediately in the situation. I carried my feelings away and hid them and when it was too late, I couldn't say how I felt. I made a huge promise to myself at fifty that I would not cast my intuition aside any more. When I need to face something important and make a decision, it would be timely and I would not avoid conflict or conviction just because. I would not shove it deep inside of me just to make the people around me comfortable.

I did this exercise about fifteen years ago, where I asked my closest friends what words they would use to describe me. It was during one of my intense periods of therapy and I found clarity on how I was perceived, to be really helpful. I even asked some of my closest employees at the time – the answers were not entirely surprising, although I was truly pleased that some respondents described me using softer and unexpected words like "caring, compassionate, nurturing," and even "sensitive."

I just repeated this exercise in July 2018. I asked two of my closest friends who have known me for over twenty years to use two words to describe me…the first words out of their mouths were "uncompromising" and "direct." Back up fifteen years and the words used were "tenacious," "ambitious," "strong," and "forthcoming."

You see, for the longest time I've wanted people to view me as balanced – strong and sensitive, assertive and thoughtful, determined and fair. Although, the reality is that most people in my life see me as a dragon, instead of a dragonfly, I sometimes secretly wish that I could be a butterfly – but only sometimes. The fact is that since my mid-forties, something inside me switched and tenacity and ambition evolved into purpose and direction. I suppose it had to do with me facing my self-imposed end to corporate life. I loved that chapter but it was time to move on and find something new that would allow me to learn continuously.

In my business life, I loved the "giving" I provided through my consultancy and expertise to clients, through my mentorship to my staff, and through my collaboration with professional partners. However, I was tired from giving and felt stagnated. My personal growth and development had stopped some years back. My need for another purpose and direction stemmed from that place where I viewed my world as being at a standstill, and I felt that the faces turned towards me had hands outstretched with palms upward. I felt and saw very few palms turned inward or downward to fill me!

In my forties, I started paying more attention to words like surrender, vulnerability, love, self, permission, and balance. For too long, I had not been the priority and I made everyone and everything else the primary focus. The pressure I put on myself to excel and exceed is too great. I was wearing myself out and would extinguish too early at this rate.

Surrender and stop worrying about the little things; they do not matter. We are all ridiculous at times, and living happily with each other means accepting all the parts that make us unique and different. "Stop worrying about little things…" Easier said than done. I have to somehow turn this into a mantra so I can bring it onboard like a comfortable cloak regularly. It's not a natural state for me but I know I can work with it and create new habits.

When I met my second husband, I was a successful entrepreneur, a respected business leader, and on top of my game in the communication world. I was partnering with the world's third largest communication group and I was choosing my clients. My team and the culture we built were spectacular, and I am supremely proud of the relationships I fostered and how successful my staff have all been during their time with me and after.

I was managing and growing my communication agency successfully, but after two decades of advising clients and being on the forefront of new business pitches, developing proposals, motivating and building teams, and essentially working eighty to ninety hours most weeks, it was time for me to consider alternatives. I loved my professional life and all that it gave me. I felt alive in business. My clients fed my soul – crazy and absolutely true.

When I decided to get remarried, it was for security, peace of mind that I would have a loyal companion in my latter years. I knew that I was getting closer to retirement and that I would be seeking a new frontier for my next productive chapter. For me, retirement meant from communication agency and corporate life, not from being active and mentally stimulated. Also, I recognized the importance to leverage my gift of effective communication and being a trusted and successful advisor to international brands for two decades. The words "empty nester" makes my skin crawl and I am certainly not ready for golf and gardening at the expense of retiring my brain.

My big fails so far:

- Education: I was far too impatient in high school. I wanted to get out into the world and start earning my own money as quickly as possible. I could say that my home and economic situation influenced my decision, but it came down to me. I decided that I couldn't/wouldn't invest the years I needed to go to university. I did not consider how a formal education could impact and even speed up the pace for me to build my career and my earning potential. Instead, I invested those early years working and finding my niche, while steadily building my earning from a lower base (without the validation of a university degree).

- Job change: I was working with an international agency where I had grown the office successfully from one client to an important regional hub in SE Asia, one employee to five, and highly profitable – in just two years. There was a great deal of respect from peers, satisfaction and pride for myself, and buckets of learning. I wanted more too soon… I scandalously agreed to lead another agency, with a bigger title and more money. Although I learned a lot, I was embarrassed that the money was not worth it after all. Had I stayed with what I had already started to build so beautifully, I would have seen a lot more rewards come tumbling through the door because I had already completed the "heavy lifting." Once I entered into negotiations to leave, I allowed too much of my pride and ego to direct me.

- Handling rejection: I remember a very special role that I applied for and was super-excited because it would get me into the luxury brand industry, which I dearly wanted to experience. Despite two fabulous interviews and excellent feedback, I was sent the most disturbing and surprising rejection letter. I reacted and my inexperience screamed too loudly. I wrote back to the firm and till now, I cringe when I think of how unprofessional my action and my words were.

- Asking for help: The first few presentations I made to potential clients (we were in a pitch situation), I was incredibly nervous. My voice box closed to a squeak, and I was perspiring. My team was with me and we had all prepared together for the pitch; I could have handed the presentation over to them comfortably to step in. However, I felt it necessary to bear the full weight of those presentations because of a misguided sense of responsibility as the lead in the agency. Collectively, just as we had developed the ideas, we could have presented it perfectly, had I relinquished some control and invited support instead.

- Safety first always: I was a new diver and we were exploring the blue waters off Krabi, Thailand. My buddy asked if I would proceed with the dive after he felt the strength of the cross current in the ocean, about one km from the beach. I should have known better and I should have answered accordingly. Instead, I proceeded with the dive against my better judgment. I was moved by the powerful current like a seaweed far off the dive coordinates, and twenty minutes into the dive I was breathless and my tank was almost out of air. There was a moment of panic and I kicked myself ruthlessly for putting my safety and that of my buddy's at risk, because I didn't say "no."

- Business protocol: I lost a very large contract when I demonstrated arrogance and contacted a senior level collaborator without the express permission of a would-be client. To add insult to injury, this was in a market where hierarchy and procedure is of critical importance and I knew that! My eagerness and inexperience did not recognize or respect the professional boundary and protocol that had to be considered, and it cost my firm dearly. It was a very hard slap in the face that stung for a long while. I had to regain respect from several parties.

- Balancing act: The ability to be a successful consultant, trusted advisor, and collaborator with clients relies on a fine balance, which allows the client their due respect as the brand guardians and experts in their industries. Although consultants and advisors are invited to participate in their businesses, we must understand that it takes trust and credibility, built over time. I had to learn to bite my tongue, after I spoke too frankly in client meetings – which naturally resulted in me losing some opportunities. With practice and deep breathing, I learned to hold criticisms and accepted the clients' decisions as final. I have entered into many heated arguments about taking risks and running innovative campaigns, but ultimately, the challenges that clients present, when they make decisions and set parameters, is part of the service provider's predicament and we can transform that into something quite satisfying when we solve the puzzle.

- Boundaries: I have miscalculated on several occasions when it came to setting and maintaining boundaries with friends, colleagues, and employees. With friends, it surrounded personal situations and I overstepped my role to be supportive; instead, I allowed my perspective to shadow my judgment of the situation and I offered too much by way of advice and opinions. With colleagues and employees, as things are in a corporate environment, it is what the culture dictates – sometimes more formal and at other times less. In my less sure and early days as a senior manager, it took some learning for me to understand how to receive and build mutual respect. I had to deal with several serious flare-ups in the agencies I managed, after employees became too comfortable with our relationship. While I endorse a cohesive and flat organizational structure, I recognize the necessity to promote and adhere to a strict reporting hierarchy.

- Face the music, face the fire: As part of being brave to want more responsibilities and more rewards, it's necessary to be prepared to face adversity and misadventures. It comes hand in hand and frankly, without the trials and miscalculations, the rewards may well be less sweet. Although I detest confrontation and will avoid it as much as possible, I adapted to handling conflict with a cool head and a diplomatic tongue. I faced many disgruntled clients and employees over my career and some situations ended in severe strife – detrimental to the relationships. It hurt emotionally and mentally to deal with such circumstances, and it's an important part of becoming a fair and reasonable business leader.

- Uncompromising: A thread that weaves through all aspects of my life – easier to step back now, with some maturity, to consider other perspectives and access empathy when necessary. As a hungry, ambitious, and goal-oriented professional, I resembled a bull with horns that only saw red capes. I am not a bully, but I am extremely focused in my actions and how I communicate. In fact, my writing style has developed in the past twenty years directly from the way I speak. I am concise and aim for clarity. In speaking to my life partners, I said things that could have been verbalized more thoughtfully. I regret many instances where I lacked consideration and compassion. Along with coaching and the reflection I've had on relationships after my recent divorce, I am proceeding with care and extreme caution.

How Do We Measure Grit and Success?

When do we know we're pushing beyond resilience, and how can we be sure we've been brave? Is there a deeper feeling of satisfaction when we've faced the crap in our lives and come out on top? How do we even pick which battles...?

As with most things in our lives, experience and recognizing patterns can be very useful. We tend to share similar challenges with each other in many ways yet the lessons we take away can be immensely varied. I put this down to perspectives; as unique as our fingerprints, we can marvel as how someone else views or handle a situation as compared to us.

Your resilience and ability to push beyond to feel the hunger in your belly and demonstrate grit, in order to overcome a challenge or achieve a tough goal, will not look like someone else's. Even your opinion of the challenges you face or what you consider a tough goal is uniquely different. There is no judgment to be made on the size and complexity of these things. Our lives are sprinkled with sufficient incidents for us all to learn from each other and value the lessons we decide to share.

My own failures and repeated challenges are somewhat universal but some are specific to my background and upbringing. For example, my experience working in my parents' shop as a child – I've never met someone else who shared that; my parents splitting when I was ten years old – many people share this history; workplace challenges as I settled into new environments with new colleagues – a universal experience; the degree to which I researched Singapore employers and the business and cultural landscape when applying for jobs – this has become more relevant as more young people travel the world looking for employment opportunities outside their own countries the past decade.

It is through my volunteer work with the Immigrant Employment Council of British Colombia (IEC-BC), SUCCESS Canada, and Kitsilano Neighborhood House that I meet diverse groups of new immigrants, and I am able to find out as much as I have about the services we offer in Canada. From settlement benefits, professional skills support and training, the different tiers of immigration, to what a fantastic role our community centers and neighborhood houses play in providing many vital programs for spouses and children to have an immediate group of friends and feel part of a community. Without the programs, I believe so many more immigrants would feel isolated and it would be much harder for them to motivate themselves each week to get out there with resumes in hand, smiling and dealing with job interviews.

My volunteer work with my nearby Kitsilano Neighborhood House has opened my eyes in so many glorious ways. I am sure, many volunteers before me found great satisfaction in their work...but perhaps not many have written about their impact. I have the privilege of listening to and exploring the bravery, resilience, and sheer enthusiasm of multicultural women from all continents share amongst each other, their commitment to make a brand new city (Vancouver) their home. They leave cherished relationships behind and seek out new ones, establish friendships in new neighborhoods, and spend tireless hours smiling and sometimes covering extreme frustrations and sadness, to follow spouses who are posted here for work.

It's a remarkable gift to witness the strength with which these families pursue their new life in Canada. The women who attend the community programs do not have the benefit of going to an office to meet colleagues and potential new friends; their days are spent with contractors and service providers turning their new rental into a home, and otherwise meeting strangers in the community. They deal with differences in the schools and help their children to settle and integrate. I spend more time around the women and few of the men come to the neighborhood house for support. They spend more time applying for jobs and getting down to the hard task of securing an income. Some of the women eventually end up applying for jobs depending on their visa situations.

In my work with immigrant professionals, both men and women who come from varied backgrounds including engineers, IT specialists, marketers, medical technicians, and trade services, I can genuinely see how driven they are. They work tirelessly to establish a new life as if they have nothing and everything to lose. I've witnessed this over and over. Their hunger is admirable and unshaken and they turn every stone in getting to their goals.

Their purpose and tenacity resonates with me because it was the way in which I moved across the world in my mid-twenties (from the Caribbean to Asia). Armed with a soul full of hope and determination, my husband and I landed in a foreign culture ready to take on the great adventure of setting up our lives. It was magical and to this day, I am so very proud of what we achieved with our bravery. It feels like I am completing a sacred circle in my work with immigrants here in Vancouver; it brings me a great deal of contentment.

The good nature with which my multicultural women's group has handled their experiences, achievements and setbacks, the past year has inspired me and it feels close to me. I plan to write about their stories in detail, how they use humor and good nature to see their challenges through the soft lens they choose to wear as they integrate into a new country.

How each person views and measures something that has to be done is linked to the way they see success. There is a direct correlation between effort and achievement. I am not wholly convinced that "no pain, no gain" applies to everything we do. We choose which fights we get into (mostly) and accordingly, we choose how much we put into it considering the upside. Being human, we mostly look for some type of reward at the end of it. It could be personal satisfaction or kudos from our peers; whatever floats our boats we consciously work better when someone has noticed.

At the end of day, it is our own egos and sense of contentment and accomplishment that has to be satisfied. We have the ability to recognize when we are working hard and admitting to it, as well as admitting to cruising and not giving a toss but going through the motions. Our realization could happen instinctively or it could take place in hindsight; our brain can do amazing things when trying to protect us from our inner voice and destructive criticism.

Success and satisfaction are states that are in constant flux within us. I can tell when I am being unduly harsh with myself – but rarely do I recognize it during my own beatings. It might be quite soon after or it could be many days…but there is the admission of guilt and regret when it's obvious that I've been driving myself nuts, working very hard to get somewhere with a particular issue, and burning my tires out of sheer frustration. After I have calmed my nerves, done a complete check-in, only then I can review my effort versus gain and make a smart decision on the best way forward or whether I want to continue with it.

Is there a deeper lesson when we push harder? I can tell when I've moved from being seriously determined to fearlessly audacious, and I can control that in myself. The personal satisfaction after I've accomplished a tough challenge is what drives me, and I love the sensation of switching gears, along with the chemicals, which flood my brain as added fuel.

New Purpose and
Shared Values

I found a wonderful ally in London when I lived in the UK – a gracious and kind CEO at one of the larger charities; she made several introductions after our meeting. Intentional networking and personal face-to-face impact is ever so meaningful, particularly when you prepare and demonstrate persistence. Through my business training over the years, I have a keen commitment to timely follow-up.

With everyone I met in the UK, whom I identified could be helpful in pushing me out to meet others, I talked at length to share my value and experience. I was transparent about my intentions with regard to living in the UK, how I could apply my vast brand communication expertise, and what I saw as a critical niche in the charity sector after reading the local newspapers. I was spot on and many shared more insight on the sector. I treated my new situation much like a client would share their position and brand challenges and from there, the launch pad to introductions and getting below the surface to meeting others who would welcome my help. These steps helped me to get off the starting line.

Each day, I read and honed in on various aspects of the different perspectives on how charities were achieving their mission and the myriad of difficulties they faced – from securing funding to attracting and retaining passionate and competent staff, to standing out from others in the sector, to what they saw as their key priorities, and how they stayed on mission. All in all, I used my professional expertise to drill right down to their key challenges – what they were saying, how, and could they continue to deliver their programs to benefit the people who needed them: in a word, sustainability.

I felt ready and motivated myself to establish a new path that would get me into the community I would now call home. Determination and grit took over and clarity stepped up. I knew that not having school-aged children in the local schools or going to a job with colleagues, both of which immediately immerses people to new acquaintances, meant a bit more legwork on my part.

While my husband went off to work each day, I filled my days with new adventures – a mix of purposeful "work" and soul-filling countryside jaunts and city exploration. Commitment is the key in everything we seek to do, isn't it? With a clear sense of purpose, we can find the energy and motivation to get to the next step, and the next, and the next. Some days, of course, there is a natural tiredness and motivation can wane, but with a genuine intention to get to a place of "this is the next stage for me," it's a chest-expanding, sensational excitement to achieve each little step forward.

As I volunteered my time with charities, I engaged board members, directors, and frontline staff. I wanted to make a positive impact while finding out as much as I could from people who were in these organizations. Just because I was new to the sector and new to the country, it did not matter because of my informed enthusiasm and curiosity. Just as I conversed with people, I listened intently. I asked a lot of questions and drew on my communication skill to bottom-line the facts in this fascinating sector.

I am truly grateful I had the opportunity to work with a charity that helps young people who struggle with mental health issues. Their programs, created by youth in the communities with the help of psychologists, provide support and guidance to prevent the same demographic from joining street gangs and from reoffending. It's a tough mandate and the charity has delivered highly effective programs for over ten years. With my involvement, the Board and front line team examined and revised its communication. In order to leverage its best practices and expand its reach to benefit more inner city youth faster, we developed a new strategy and toolkit for everyone to speak less clinically about the charity's work, and to outline its redefined role as a facilitator.

While there is so much to be said for how charities operate, not just in the UK but globally, and how much can be improved, the work that is led by passionate visionaries and volunteers astound me each week. The programs that make a real impact to strangers living across the globe are not to be scoffed at, and it takes hundreds if not thousands of people working together consistently and committedly to make a difference.

I went through my phase of researching how much of the public's contributions made to various global charities actually make it to the small villages and villagers, and I have my top list of "they pay their administrators far too much." However, on the grand scheme of things, I have decided that even the charities who spend too much on their directors and administration, contribute something to their benefactors and that's the key. The charities that pay their directors and administrators a higher salary versus others who push most of their funding back into their services and mission are still making an impact. Reduced dollars are better than zero dollars for charitable purposes.

At many gatherings, dinner parties, discussions over my lifetime so far, I listen and look at the faces of people who talk about the dreadful outfits who spend too much on salaries and "nothing gets utilized for the greater good." These people have the luxury of speaking from a warm room with a delicious drink in hand and a spread of food in front of them. The reality is that many charities will continue to work very hard to deliver their programs however, unless they keep evolving their strategies and using some of the valuable dollars to attract talented people to the sector, they will fold and will not be able to sustain any of their work. In the end, consider which scenario is better?

The concept of values and purpose is overtly popular now. It's gone from a question that privileged, and sometimes more emotionally aware people asked each other, to a spike in reality and in general discussions at the water cooler. While it's fantastic that more people ask these questions of themselves and each other, I feel it's lost a deeper impact because people are thinking mostly of HOW to answer the question. My observation is that many are having these conversations because they want to feel good about it being part of their story – yet, the actions necessary to demonstrate they are embracing purpose are yet to be seen.

It can be argued that more people find it easier to identify their values…from their parents and upbringing, and even from teachers and learning from friendships. I would also challenge that what is morally valuable to people is rarely communicated publicly. Values are wide-ranging and not meant to be correct or even similar for people who spend time together. Your values are as special as your thinking and thought process – whether from nature or nurture.

Purpose on the other hand is a fascinating topic for me. I only became aware of true purpose, my purpose, at two distinct times in my life. And I am well aware that my purpose will continue to evolve with age and experience. As I create opportunities to make the impact I wish to make, I will identify with my purpose differently over time; knowing myself, I will explore what resonates in my heart and head and I will reflect on it to make the necessary adjustments. I am not suggesting this is for everyone. A purpose-led life can be a tougher path to take and it requires genuine commitment to truth and a wide, open perspective.

Just as I have coached many clients, the truth to identify what you are good at and what you're unable to do is a matter of self-admission. There is no admission of failure – absolutely everyone has a different skillset and passion. The fact that we are encouraged to work together as teams must mean something. To help each other personally and professionally, collaboration could become second nature if we truly embrace diversity in what each of us can do. No one would be left to struggle with differences in approach or the lack of an ability in a certain area, because we can then ask for help without embarrassment or fear of judgment.

Purpose and perspective for me go hand in hand. Sometimes as I make a subconscious decision, I have to try hard to recognize if there is a bias and if there is, I consider whether sticking with that decision is the right thing for me or whether I'm being lazy.

Coaching and Mentorship Is a Priceless Gift

I started out seeking coaching for me, as I was launching myself into retirement (or so I thought) and asking questions about my second chapter. How could I continue to be useful, make an impact and help people somehow, and grow? I cannot stagnate otherwise, I feel like there is a heavy bag over my face pushing me downwards under water. Whatever I do, and for the people around me, I must feel like I am growing just as I am impacting their lives. It's not a financial reward; it's a feeling of mutual gain and resonance. It's how I walk away from someone and a situation feeling like we did something special for each other in the exchange of information, insight, integrity, and honesty.

If you've ever had a feeling of euphoria or deep fulfillment speaking to a mentor or a coach – you'll know what I refer to – the fireworks that fly in one's brain after such a great exchange is powerful beyond words. This type of symbiotic relationship can extend to partners, colleagues, friends and general companions, but it seems harder to maintain on a consistent level with life partners. Perhaps it's the subconscious setting of states and rules that takes over after familiarity sets in; we cannot seem to allow a completely even and equal relationship to be.

I pushed beyond resilience and tenacity at different times, in order to make a success of my life. I knew that I wanted to live outside the West Indies; it had no future for me because I was very ambitious and saw myself enjoying a lot more. My sense of adventure extends to how I live, the people I want to spend my time with, the food I enjoyed, and the environments in which I immerse myself. I consider my grit to come from a mix of my father's incredible DNA – how he traveled across the globe in a fishing trawler as a young man escaping a vicious war in Vietnam, to create a life on the edge of South America not speaking a word of the language, coupled with personal ambition and sheer drive. My determination for achieving my goals was carved in stone like commandments in my mind – ticking off one at a time.

When I began my journey with coaching, I listened and learned the most incredible truths about myself. At the time I considered myself hyperaware of me and yet, there was so much more. Layers were peeled away and I found a greater meaning of "genuine." The other reality that presented itself was that the classroom was filled with people from around the world, from different parenting and cultural backgrounds, yet, we were all the same AND we were all different. Cliché and oh so true! We had the same fears and dealt with them differently; we had the same personality traits yet they were expressed uniquely; we had the same desires and went about fulfilling them similarly and differently.

It was a unifying program to say the least, to understand that beneath the surface of our skin we were human beings finding our places. I took to coaching immediately and I loved the discomfort it caused me. I grew an inch each time we had a new module. During the course, I decided that I would complete the full accreditation program to offer this gift to others and become a professional coach. It was another tool in my valuable toolbox for my second chapter and I felt immensely pleased. It felt right.

Personally, coaching provided a topper to the therapy I'd had the last nineteen years. At various points in my life, I sought a deeper understanding of what was coursing through my brain and why I was feeling what I did. I remember each period acutely. It's been a great help to me not just to write during the really crap times in my life, but then to analyze my confusion and perspectives with a therapist and make more scribbles during the exploration and dissection.

Over the twenty-two years, I worked in communication and marketing with clients and building businesses, I realize just how much mentorship I've received and provided throughout the years and to such a wide variety of nationalities. I have loved every opportunity and I hope I made the good impact that I feel I have made. Building on that experience my coaching is now providing so much more...to me and to the people I'm working with.

My niche has come about holistically and that's the best way I feel. When I set out to coach various clients right after my training, I felt capable, but with some clients, I did not feel a deep connection. Now, I work with international students at the University of British Columbia, new immigrants through charity foundations, and women at the neighborhood house, as well as business owners who ask for a wake-up call on their focus, direction, and commitment to be successful (and that means different things to different clients). Recently, I am coaching more ambitious career professionals who recognize they could use a resolute sounding board, to address their bravery and commitment to honoring who they are and to bring that to the forefront.

I feel my chest thumping in a good way. I know I am providing coaching and mentorship to a group of people who really want to dig deeper to lead more successful lives (by their definitions), and I am working with clients who are hungry to create new opportunities and to find their purpose.

I am a firm believer that one way for us all to pay forward our gifts is to provide mentorship. This does not have to take the form of a fixed, formal relationship. Sometimes just speaking with someone regularly, checking in, and most of all, listening, can be the most rewarding gift of all. I've been practicing listening and observation from a young age and I encourage everyone, with and without children in their lives, to spend more time silently observing. Silently pay attention because there is so much to take in – the most detailed canvas can be created with the active listening that's possible amongst all of us. And the things we find out about ourselves in the process – priceless. It's not listening to categorize and judge, nor is it listening to place value. Our similarities and our differences are spectacular and they make our lives intricately unique yet familiar. I listen to understand and accept.

My recent pet peeve is noticing that people listen just barely enough to respond. It seems that before someone can complete their sentence, the facing party has an urgent delivery to make with a view to sharing a similar or competing story. If it's the one thing you can change about the way in which you listen to people, listen with every sense you have – don't listen just to say something or to show a bit of empathy. Listen and feel, and appreciate just how much information is being shared with you.

While coaching requires a professional qualification, the ability to mentor is in all of us to share because we have lived and learned. We all have stories and have had some impact made on us by parents, relatives, friends, teachers, and our children. These stories and the impact we share are all critical contributions in making us understand and accept diversity and it can promote a way of collaboration that is universal to mitigate cultural barriers.

I Discovered Hugs
and Oxytocin

As a child growing up with Asian parents, in the West Indies, hugs were rare. Human touch was centered more around discipline – even from teachers. Sounds like I grew up in the dark ages but no, this was in the seventies – when I attended primary school. That's how recent corporal punishment was accepted and practiced in the school system in parts of the world.

My early, most endearing memories of hugs came with friends. We hugged each other intently when we met for drinks after work, or at the end of the night going home, or dropping in to each other's homes for a meal. We somehow without words, dived in for tight hugs. I have to admit there are some brilliant huggers out there – they are just a natural!!! I am lucky and I have several people in my life that fit this description… Their hugs are to die for. My toes curl and I feel the wind in my sails – it's the most incredible sensation in the whole world. Sometimes, it is far beyond the satisfaction that one can get from an orgasm.

When I read about oxytocin in my thirties, it made so much sense. Through various stages in my life when I was grieving, I felt that this powerful chemical was the only thing that lifted me from the murky, thick waters of despair. A warm and loving pair of arms around me could melt fears and anguish instantly. If you haven't tried this, I urge you to do it for someone. Only by giving it unconditionally, you can get it back without reservation. People tend to melt and even collapse into great hugs and it's a mutual tank-filler. Someone might swoop in for a hug thinking they are giving you one, but if you can reciprocate with unbridled warmth, you will blow their socks off and you get so much in return.

As you can read I love hugs, and I tell myself every week to get even better at it. I want to give more hugs and give myself the permission to show that emotion and feel it come right back. I visualize a large boomerang swooping across a gorgeous canyon, touching every beautiful corner and picking up all that it can from the air and nature, and pinging it right back at me. I am not able to meditate in the traditional sense but by creating these vivid pictures in my thoughts, I can relax and calm my mind when I feel the need. By sharing time with people I enjoy, we fill each other's depleted reservoirs while having fun.

Have you watched the way in which kids hug and play with each other? When parents say, "Look, it's Julie, give her a hug." The joy on their faces and the gleeful gurgles they make is one of unbridled happiness. Every inch of their bodies resonate and shake with happiness. Why do we lose this and how can we consciously regain it as adults? Surely, we are intelligent enough to understand the importance of such love and surely, we can adapt in order to give and receive it? I often joke we're the stupidest animals on the planet…even with the gift of language.

There is something that happens temporarily with new parents, newlyweds, new relationships. Our brains seem to register the importance of sustaining connection and we enjoy giving and receiving oxytocin during this period of newness. Once the relationships are familiar however, something seems to change. A thin coat of lack-luster enters the equation and less effort is made to engage and excite one another. With our children of course, this is different – but still, I have noticed how sheer excitement can wane and reality steers the way.

With the coming-of-end in my romantic relationships over time, I've put a lot more equity into my friendships. I hug, I listen, I make a conscious effort to be fully present, and I take my responsibility as a friend seriously. I want these relationships to last a lifetime – they feed me and hopefully, I feed my friends.

Do I wish I could have fed and received more oxytocin from my life partners? You bet I do. However, for various reasons our passion for each other dwindled and excitement was more work than mutual reward. You might judge and think "cold." However, these are particular crossroads where I see so many people ignoring their basic, vital needs, and sticking to what's familiar. Moving forward and facing our reality alone is hard for many compared to staying in what might be disharmonious but still comfortable. Even though we may not be getting what we need on a regular basis to thrive, change is a hard nut to crack and chew for many.

The excuse that people stay together for the sake of their children has long been over-used, and the flipside that many do not make a significant effort to preserve their relationships because we are faced with more and easier options do not bode well with me either. Every individual has the right to pursue the love they want – compromise, although necessary in some areas in life, may not apply well here because we end up with a flame buried inside that singes something vital over time.

Be bold in admitting to yourself and your suitors what kind of love you wish to have and who you are as a partner or lover. Overwhelming passion and desire, lustful looks from each other, or quiet walks hand in hand – whatever style of loving you want and give, be true in communicating that to ensure you have a connection with someone who is compatible. This aspect of a relationship is frequently hidden behind other priorities, which seem to be flaunted more easily, like mutual respect, honesty, sense of humor, blah, blah. Great chemistry in and outside the bedroom is heavenly and we all deserve it, particularly if society expects us to be monogamous. Respect, honesty, and a good giggle from time to time add to the magic; there is no doubt!

Communication and Honesty

To be fair, I do communicate openly about my necessary desires when I meet someone. However, I observe that my dates feel compelled to match or level up on those things. Are they honest with themselves and with me right from the start? At some point, due to a fake façade at the beginning of dating and miscommunication for the first few months, things end up in a real state. What would be the brave thing to do? What would you do?

The decision to part ways is hard and one that takes particular courage when it affects more than two people. Friends and relatives are hard hit when couples split. Children, of course, are the primary concern due to the pain and adjustment they often struggle with for many years. I have lost and gained friendships after each of my three splits from long-term partners, and I learned more lessons about the way in which others, particularly relatives, face disruption and change.

We are humans and the state of being includes the need to be hugged, touched, kissed, and satisfied sexually. I have spoken to many friends over the past twenty years and I know they push these things away, but from time to time, the lava bubbles… There is a ticking time bomb in some that could damage unsuspecting bystanders quite severely. Men and women carry immense guilt for just imagining what could be different if they ended their stale relationships and started anew. I have personally squashed my own desires from time to time, but I could not sustain a celibate lifestyle, nor could I participate in dull, routine lovemaking, with no personal satisfaction.

Some may well argue that I place too much importance on the pleasures of the flesh – I think not. I know many women and men, who require a satisfying and robust sex life as they do air. While both men and woman share this basic need, my observation and research amongst my peers tell me more women do not admit to its importance in their lives.

Honesty with ourselves and open communication with people around us together, are a rare beauty and I crave more of it. In many of my sessions with therapists and coaches, I listen to myself and others talking about the need to have honesty, to receive, and to give it. Like my own experience in the past, it seems that many relationships suffer because openness takes a conscious effort and even more commitment to sustain throughout our years with partners.

It's easier in the early days, or after a fight and discussion, or when we share the responsibility for a young child, and some may say in second marriages. But in the day to day of a familiar long-term relationship when it's "life" keeping us busy – responsibilities, childcare, routines, and the steady rigor of jobs, the open communication which would normally accompany a new love adventure slips away ever so slowly and steadily. What can we do to pull it back regularly? Importantly, what can we do to remain honest with what we want as we share our lives with a companion?

Too often we lie to ourselves about what we want, who we really are, and how we feel. It's how we stop living in a way that embraces our values, and many live smaller than their worth to keep the peace. If the goal is to "not rock the boat," can this work for long-term happiness and contentment? With constant lies to ourselves about who we are and what we want, we have to extend those lies to the people around us. This is why I have made many of the seemingly selfish decisions I've made – not to run away from a bad situation, but to be a better person, a better mother, and a better friend. I could not stay true to partners and still be thriving if my soul was not fed and my heart rate did not race once in a while. It would be impossible to sustain without harsh resentment and consequences.

The honesty, with which we view our values and ourselves, goes up and down with personal situations. I believe that few are able to consciously see themselves without rosy-colored glasses on a consistent basis. Perhaps it's survival mode on some level. Perhaps that's just how our brain works to protect us. I love checking in with myself regularly – to tear away any illusions that might be starting to form. For me, that's keeping myself in check and real. I am my best critic and I don't wear velvet gloves when I remove my comfort cloak. It's an ongoing challenge to be genuine, and to admit, when something has to be shifted. In my twenties and thirties, I'd blurt out more often when something in me is not genuine – something my coach training has reminded me of the past few years...to acknowledge and say things in the moment as I see it.

This is a particularly valuable area in which my coaching and mentorship help people. As an intrepid coach, I challenge my clients and I tell them this about my coaching style upfront. I am not hired to be their friend and the advice which friends and relatives provide for people are mostly based on love, caring, and protection – part opinion and reality. I do not provide advice. My role, as a professional coach, is to help clients look at many different perspectives while peeling away the layers which protect and avoid harsh truths to be considered.

We set rules without even thinking about it and ignore our own shortcomings. We tend to assume a superior position and some accept those rules even though it does them a great disservice. It's one way of establishing a hierarchy subconsciously with our peers. It worked for me for many years in my early career days but once I had a semblance of who my true adult self was, my gifts, and what resonated with the people around me when I was real, I embraced the genuine woman I am. I am stubborn and I have an acute lack of patience with ignorance. I am sometimes, a bull in a china shop and speak my mind in a very direct manner. Oh yes, and I have a serious deficit in understanding overpowering nationalism and protectionist views.

I have parented my daughter to see things for what they are and, where possible, to have a voice. As an only child, she spent her years growing up with adults, my friends and me around the dinner table. We still gather and talk, laugh, and share stories candidly – love and camaraderie evident throughout her years, with children having their roles in the conversations. It's what feels natural in our home and it's how we went beyond parent and child, to having a relationship that is wide open and full of respect, admiration and connection. We disagree vehemently about things sometimes, and it's a way of learning about the other individual. I want to know whom my young daughter will grow into, and I want her to know who I am beyond being her mother. As a young woman, she has demonstrated remarkable resilience and I can't wait to see her hunger for the things she want in her adult life.

Our communication over the years has transcended mother-daughter language. We talk about things in a way that is honest and on many occasions, relatives and friends have complimented us on this achievement. There are strict boundaries in place. I am still her parent. However, we promote honesty and she is well aware of just how much I loathe lies. I suppose that is a key difference between many families and us – the ability to set and respect boundaries and still be able to speak our minds openly to each other. I respect her boundaries and yet I push like a protective parent. When it feels right, we proceed together or we back off. She understands my boundaries and as a young child, she most definitely pushed, and now that she is a young woman, she balances understanding with self-exploration and respect for her mom.

When I coach clients who are business owners, I ask them to admit if they started the firm in order to make money. There is no guilt whatsoever in acknowledging that a healthy profit is what propelled you to become an entrepreneur in the first place. While philanthropy is beautiful, it's not the end goal for everyone. Relative materialism and enjoying the peace of mind that money brings are valid requirements and great goals to have. Others can judge this harshly but the reality is we need money to experience some of the glorious things that make our lives joyful and happy. As I write this book, I am coming away from an incredible bucket-list sailing holiday. It took some planning because I was intent on making it happen and now, I have the most amazing memories of sailing around the Adriatic and driving through wild mountain ranges in the Balkans. I wouldn't have been able to do this without money.

The Corporate Soldier and Values

In the latter part of my corporate years, I asked others and myself this question repeatedly – is there an inherent conflict when we commit ourselves to doing what's necessary in a company with the intention 'for profit.' This is assuming that by the time we are in our mid-thirties, we have identified some values that resonate frequently.

At some point, you may have to ask yourself if you are in the right industry and if the company you work for, is a good fit. This is a very difficult enquiry for many because we are faced with reality – living expenses may well dictate what you do and how much discomfort you're willing to accept; natural capabilities may put us at a disadvantage to choose, or you could love what you're doing despite the emotional clash.

My earliest job was in marketing coordination – i.e. I assisted a marketing director to ensure things were organized and that all pieces of communication and logistics were lined up for campaigns. I had the good fortune to work with external partners such as the advertising firm who put together the content for what we were selling. With time, I became experienced and better at my role and I was put in charge of deciding what our ads would say. This was the beginning of when I paid careful attention to the written word.

Two jobs later, I joined a public relations firm and was introduced to that aspect of publicity. As part of a global agency and with a robust and fast-growing practice in Southeast Asia, which in itself was a hotbed for business in the late eighties, I learned new things on a daily basis. Importantly, I understood the difference between public relations and advertising; the use of words and credibility in its delivery significantly impact consumers (arguably, even more so today). I fell in love with the mastery of building public relationships and the sheer power of communication.

Fast-forward ten years: I grew exponentially as a communication consultant and advisor for clients across the region and I was engaged on many occasions to directly advise their advertising firms on key messaging. My brain was adept at developing the words that would engage people's attention and invite curiosity. This was for me and for my successful business that would follow, a critical skill I continued to develop and shape for another decade and a half. Moreover, I loved my industry – the outcome I witnessed and the relationships I developed with editors and journalists over time became a source of pride and peppered great discussions.

Public relations also taught me to be highly professional and to have integrity – what we wrote twenty-five years ago could not be fake, slanderous, or boastful. There was acute attention to trustworthiness and reputation and everyone respected this rule. There were no bloggers; journalists were revered and editors treated like the gatekeepers of reputation heaven. As a PR consultant, it was my job to explore and write pieces of content, or at least pitch that idea of a headline to a journalist, on behalf of my clients. I was harshly criticized by my boss if I didn't conduct sufficient research, share facts, used language that was engaging, and fulfilled just the right word count so that the media outlet I was targeting would readily accept the piece for their readers. I had a tough boss and she drove me hard; I learned a lot and I blossomed.

Although I hadn't identified specific values at that stage, I knew instinctively that what I wrote or pitched for a story in a newspaper or magazine was built on truth and trust. I was very happy with my job as a result because I wasn't pushing words that were filled with empty promises.

The way that my industry has evolved the past fifteen years, with the importance of bloggers and vloggers and the speed at which communication and messages are delivered – both true and false, has had a dramatic effect on credibility and how skeptical we've grown with "news." The shift to personal, peer-to-peer critique and recommendation is more important and even bloggers run the risk of extinction as our mistrust multiplies. I have spoken to several people in the PR industry and it's a different landscape now.

Whichever industry you're in and at whatever stage you are in admitting your values, be aware that it is you who choose. If you wish to separate your corporate and personal life so you have an easier time with conscience while fulfilling your material needs, so be it. Check in regularly with yourself. However, be sure to capture what is genuinely working for you and explore how the two spheres might work together in harmony. A job and environment that sucks the integrity out of you and demands that you spend the weekend sleeping to recover is hardly worth living.

Why Do So Many "Live Small?"

It's a term that I only heard, or at least paid attention to, the past eight years or so – but I certainly understand its implications. I observed many people around me, from my upbringing in the West Indies, to my business network across Asia, and senior professionals I've met in the UK – they perform at a level that's easy, no ruffles and no surprises. And I'm not just referring to their careers.

At some point or another, we have all been around colleagues and bosses who didn't seem to work very hard – physically or mentally. They were in the office but were they? Have you worked in the presence of someone who simply bought into everyone else's creation? People who didn't participate as far as giving ideas or even feedback, theirs was more of a constant nod and a voting presence. On the other hand, there are colleagues and bosses who light our fires – they promote an atmosphere of generosity and limitless possibilities; we feed lucratively on that plate.

If you reflect on the top five challenges you faced in your professional and personal life the past fifteen years, would you admit to demonstrating resilience, grit, or taking the easy road? What worked for you in those situations and why? Knowing what you do now about the outcome and yourself, yes hindsight, what would you choose in a "do over?" Can you call yourself resilient? When, if ever, have you demonstrated that you aren't willing to take the no-risk, quiet path to getting somewhere? What exactly do you understand by these words: living small?

People busy themselves with tasks to stay busy. They do not actually make any impact in their firms, and they barely create a ripple in their personal lives. It's a very different way of living and some choose to exist this way, while others talk about being brave but without any follow through. I have attended many meet-up events the past four years and I enjoy great banter with some of the individuals who love to discuss their take on someone else's tough situation.

Their stories almost always seem to be encircled around "but I would have" or the "what ifs." They live vicariously through other people's adventures and yet, they are adept at giving advice, despite not ever leaving their comfortable cocoons to experience the harsh conditions outside.

Personally, after a week of intense coaching about ten years ago, after my heart was broken and I needed to assess my options, I consciously listed about twenty words I would remove from my everyday vocabulary. I limit my use of "but, no, why, regret, dream," and several others. I retrained my language to be inclusive and to be a better reflection of my psychology when it comes to embracing innovation, open and different perspectives, challenges, and adventures. It was quite an exercise and I gained contentment as a result. My language is much more positive, less sarcastic, and I've regained my sense of humor.

I look at the way some people choose their jobs – what they apply for as suitable despite their innate abilities and qualifications. I have questioned some of these people and they humbly reply that they do not like pressure. They prefer to work at something safe for the rest of their lives, with just enough to be happy, without the stress of a higher paying role and responsibilities. Of course, the flipside of that thinking is that they will always be working to keep their bowl half full. Effort and achievement is inextricably tied and the reward is also on par.

The reason I raise this point is not to judge, but to highlight that those who choose to live in a comfortable zone should have a realistic view of themselves and how their lives will play out. They talk differently to the way they act; they speak of a bigger game…as if they are out hunting when in fact, they are actually gatherers and stay close to the fence around their gardens. There is value in knowing what works for each of us and how we adapt accordingly to accept and achieve that. Just as living large comes with a high price in terms of how much effort, the dedication and stamina, and responsibilities – living small against our natural instinct takes its toll.

It comes down to impact – what are your values and if you have some purpose you'd like to fulfill during your lifetime. Is the way you are living your life giving you the opportunities to make your desired impact? Why not see your living for what it is and ask yourself some tough questions? Write the answers down on a slip of paper and look at it. What emotions do those answers evoke in you? Is your movie going to make you smile?

Will Being Brave Make Us Happy?

Yes, there is something that swells in our chest, and it also makes the people witnessing our happiness, proud. That's worth it. It's how you make yourself feel. We talk about making a positive impact on others. Well, how about you?

Are you objectively able to identify when you're shrinking from a decision? When you turn a blind eye to something or talk yourself into a "safe" scenario? There is no shame in admitting that sometimes, we opt for a slow pace, to catch our breaths and to recharge. Obviously, not every situation calls for some sort of bravery. There are hundreds of decisions made every week that require no thought whatsoever, far less bravery! However, there are circumstances when you have to make a considered choice – play along to get a fair outcome, push a bit harder for a tiny wedge more, or go for the whole hog and roar like a lion. I believe we can all feel that transformation in our gut or our chest when we decide and when we proceed to show courage. It has an immediate impact on our bodies.

Question yourself if it feels good. It certainly feels great when I am brave, and by definition, I'm happy. On the other hand, whenever I've stepped back from making a bold choice, I felt different levels of regret.

Just as there are many different roles and responsibilities for people of all backgrounds and capabilities, there are varied situations for taking brave action as well as cruising in a gear that is comfortable and easy. A person may slip into a job that is such a great fit they might never really stretch themselves. Others are given opportunities to shine in a job that takes them well outside their comfort zone. Their day to day may well consist of multiple mini battles to achieve company objectives. These positions take its toll over time and it's a good idea to find the right tools to step away and restore yourself. It may well be that you flourish with this type of pressure and that you feel most creative and productive. However, try to keep a full tank in order to have the energy and stamina.

I know there are people who work just sufficiently to get by. It blows my mind but they choose to live that way and they like it. If they need some new clothes, they work extra shifts. If an unexpected expense hits them, they try not to panic. I have a mix of admiration and anxiety for such people.

At the height of my business success, I worked ninety hours a week. I was super motivated, excited by my work, and felt more alive than ever. I used five hours of sleep begrudgingly to rest and couldn't wait to get out for a run at 6 am before settling back at my laptop by 7:30. I set my hours so that I could spent 5:30 to 8 pm with my daughter throughout her elementary school years, and then got back online after she went to bed. I justified this happily because I was working with international clients across all sorts of time zones. I attended phone discussions and made presentations to suit my clients' schedules in Europe, UK, USA, Middle East, and Africa.

I rarely, if ever, said no. That period in my life was deeply satisfying in terms of what I achieved for my professional growth, my agency's reputation, and profitability. I never considered it a sacrifice and it was courageous to be that dedicated and for as long as I sustained it. It made me happy and that's why I did it.

Let's explore if we weren't brave when we needed to be. If we regularly chose to ignore the challenge and turn away, how would that pattern make us feel? Are we able to justify not achieving our goals, because we refuse to make a sustained attempt? Being in a flat-line existence could work some of the time – I see that clearly; but throughout one's lifetime, how can we thrive if we feel little to no excitement in the way we choose to live, love, work, interact, and explore?

Why Do We Benchmark?

The reality is people fulfill many different roles in society to create an economy. From the people helping us to build our homes, teaching our children, managing giant corporations, or making ice cream, we all benefit from the acceptance that everyone has a place on the giant wheel. It would further benefit all of us, and our children, if our consciousness allowed us to see equal value across these responsibilities.

The subconscious bias which exist continues to be passed from one generation to the next, and we still hear parents threatening their kids with becoming a dishwasher or a rubbish collector if they didn't study hard, or relatives gossiping about someone marrying below their status, and my favorite: "You'll be shoveling shit at the rate you're going," as if working at a farm would be so horrible!

Like ego, I believe we benchmark because it gives us something to aim for – a starting point; we can then go higher or lower and pat ourselves on the back. Without that pinpoint in our heads, we can't seem to proceed. There is an opportunity however to use this to our advantage.

If we are being brave and we honestly admit what our talents and shortcomings are, we would be able to set bold intentions knowing that we are prepared to engage others to help propel us towards our goals. There wouldn't actually be a goal that is unachievable because we'd know that despite ourselves, we would be seeking the expertise we needed to realize that intention somehow.

I have benchmarked high when it comes to quality of work, professionalism, customer satisfaction, respect, and manners. These things are supremely important to me and I drive my daughter nuts with my expectations. I still remember my mother's absurd words: "Eat properly. Pretend the Queen is coming for dinner." What the!!! However, I have been complimented on my good manners and grace on many occasions. So absurd or not, some things worm its way into our brain. On this premise, I sincerely hope that my incessant nagging on quality, pride, and honesty has not gone straight out the other ear with my daughter. She certainly deserves to be praised for some of the mature qualities she exudes already and I am immensely proud.

In business if we didn't benchmark, would there be a dip in quality? Is it necessary to refresh our minds when we set goals so that we consistently satisfy customers' demands? As intelligent humans, couldn't we self-regulate? Is that why society is governed by laws and is that what laws are – benchmarks?

The Start of My Second Chapter

Packing up and disrupting our very comfortable lives, to immigrate to the UK was a huge leap for my husband and me, two people almost fifty years old. The work involved to settle in a new country, make friends, and find a community that would be suitably nice where we feel at home...loomed larger than I wanted. I decided that for me to combine what I had done in my first career, and to fulfill my new purpose, I would dedicate my talents to the charity sector for a while.

Bravery takes on a whole new meaning when two people move continents and rely heavily on each other to build a home. There are so many moving parts and the inclination to stay well within one's comfort zone is overwhelming. However, we pushed each other to explore our new surroundings and the UK was spectacular in providing the greatest backdrop to a very different life outside of what we were used to in Asia.

The settling period was hard – we enjoyed the first few months and then pushed into gears for making our lives more permanent there. That meant scratching a bit harder beneath the surface... Countryside hikes became more peppered with reading the local newspapers to get up to speed on what was happening in our community; grocery shopping included paying close attention to prices, who was shopping there and the diversity of selection; and more time was spent finding my husband the right job in his industry given his vast experience in Asia. And of course, more intentional and purposeful networking lay ahead.

I spent my time meeting new people through hobby groups, looking at various FB pages and different-sized charities and their work and impact. It was a joy and a real blessing that charities in the UK are all so transparent in their work and I could find a ton of events and forums to attend for more information. I met incredibly interesting and dedicated people and became involved, and my husband found work. We were on our way to settling and establishing a new home.

Fortunately or unfortunately, a move from Asia also included moving away from luxuries that one gets used to over the years. I had considered this carefully before raising the possibility of a move, so I was ready to clean our house, prepare the meals, drive hubby to the train station each day, and generally become the home-based help instead of an equal contributor to our finances. My husband was not quite there in his mindset and so it took a bit of time and more adjustment for him when we had to do everything ourselves in and around the home.

This by no means is a complaint; it should be mentioned though that the reality of going from dual income and fulltime help to self-sufficiency, takes a shift in roles and active engagement to do things for each other. Easier said than done – habits take over and it takes constant reminders that shoes at the front door do not put themselves away, or the vegetables bought five days ago still exist in the fridge, and the dogs need a good walk or they will chew their paws off.

Everything people talk about – the harsh stories about making new friends when you're older and have little but your own hobbies to rely on...they are somewhat true. It takes a lot of motivation and constant effort to keep at it. Perseverance, as it works with everything else, is magical. It got me out to meet the same people somewhat regularly, walking and exploring parts of London, talking about our own experiences living in different places, and essentially sharing sufficient details about me to establish a connection. Fortunate for me, I did not connect with people who only talked about their children and education. I met wonderful, genuine people who had rich, interesting lives and we shared great stories about new cultures, food, and people. It's a universal connector – travel and adventures.

From my relatively newfound talent to be more open and chatty, I discussed my new circumstance – facing a new chapter and what others love to refer to as "empty nest syndrome." I have developed a keen dislike for that term – it sounds lifeless to me. With a keen sense of purpose, I searched for opportunities to get involved in some charities to use my communication expertise. The more I read and more networking events I attended, I realized I could use my experience with brands to help charities in several ways and timely too, when funding was a significant challenge for many.

With a larger demand for the same purse of money to be shared by governments and policymakers, and public fatigue to give, charities need to hone in on their language and delivery channels to make a greater impression on their stakeholders. From politicians to the man in the street, it is necessary for charities to resonate better and secure empathy for the programs they are delivering. It continues to be highly relevant for charities to not just "talk" about their programs but to clearly demonstrate their sustainable impact. I am committed to working with charities and in the spring of 2019, I will be spending four months in Central America with Raleigh International, as their field communication officer. I am bursting with excitement to get stuck in.

Instead of trying to leverage the friendships which hubby already had in our new country, I left it to him to re-establish his relationships after so many years abroad, while I used my professional background to create conversations with interesting, new people. My stagnant self felt alive and I could feel the fresh air in my lungs again. My chest rose and finally, for the first time in a very long while, I could identify personal growth and a real stretch.

What Else Is There?

I know what I want and I know what I don't want. I know I am open to new things and therefore, I have tossed my balls in the air to find what is right for me in this phase of my life. Where will they fall? So far I love exactly where they are landing...

I don't have the robotic data-driven analytics to avoid more potholes and mistakes and frankly, I don't wish to because it would be a flat life. I like to feel and I like the emotions that accompany taking new paths and exploring new adventures. At any age, that will be the trademark of my life – the considered easy way, versus the way to fill my life with a certain amount of excitement and learning. I am not the person who takes the most difficult path just to say I have. I simply do not follow traditional ways of doing things nor do I follow blindly. I consider my options carefully, and I look for ways to make my living awesome. I still like to feel the rush of excitement when I make a decision and when I set out on that journey.

As I play my movie in my head, I want to smile – like a glamour puss that gets a regular taste of deliciousness. My friends marvel that I do not have a single wrinkle at fifty-three. Well, I have this one deep groove that runs in the center of my forehead. It's my grand canyon of reflection and movie review – I use it often.

After I made the scary decision to be single again at fifty-one, I took a deep dive into my purpose and what I wanted for myself during this next and very important phase of my life. A few bucket-list items popped up, and combined with getting my daughter off to university and wanting to stay committed to charity work for at least 30% of my time, I knew that I would continue to have a full and busy life. For me, golf and gardening is still a long way off and I look forward to enjoying that. My perfect split is working about 40% of my time – and that means doing something I absolutely love like coaching or developing communication strategies for businesses; the other 60% equally split between self-care and charity work: hiking in deep forests or tall mountains with my thoughts, or providing professional support for new immigrants.

Writing this book is a bucket-list item. I sat at my computer in the spring of 2017, one very sunny, cold day in Vancouver, and the words just poured out. My fingers kept tapping for days and at the end of it, I had over twenty thousand words on my screen and a chest full of emotions bubbling up to my throat. I felt alive, scared, and extremely excited by the future I was about to embark on. It was a glorious affirmation that I had done the right thing to move away to my own space to start fresh.

I felt brave in making the decision and even braver in handling the logistics for another international move. However, relatives and friends silently and not so silently communicated their feelings about my decision and some days this affected me quite badly. In the words some chose and in other silent communication, I could see their disapproval with my actions. Eyes rolled and it was fairly easy to see some thinking, "Why does she want to be on her own at this age?" I grappled with that thought for quite some time and circled back to the same place. I was happier on my own than with someone with whom I felt we did not share unconditional love.

I struggled for a while to reconcile that I weighed companionship and security less important than emotional stability and contentment. I beat myself up badly for close to a year – silently, but badly. It was not a brave decision to marry again. I had shifted gears as part of my quasi-retirement and thought that cruising in third would work just fine. I also thought security was most important at that stage. For me, it didn't work because I ended up compromising on too many things and I stagnated. I stopped challenging myself, and my own self-care and joy was stretched and put at the end of the queue again. Add in all the changes to making a new life in a completely different country/culture, and being resilient took on a whole new meaning.

As part of this unsettling period, my conversations with my young daughter are playing a vital role. It's important for me to ensure this young woman I am raising understands and appreciates that human connection and relationships are the utmost priority for long-term fulfillment and happiness. Even though I have moved on from various relationships, it is important to understand that I never considered them disposable – on the contrary. I have hurt on the inside very badly and I wished, on some occasions, I could compromise more and therefore be happier with less. People and relationships are not disposable.

As part of my responsibility as a parent, I want my daughter to understand that my need to live fully, be true to who I am, and the things I wish to achieve, means that I must be extra careful in making romantic connections. The three men who have shared my life over thirty-three years have impacted my being in the most incredible ways and I have very special places in my heart that feature those stories. Using the right words to describe my journey and my decisions to her is very tough. I balance it so that she is able to see when I act on something it is done without malice. It's not me simply falling out of love; it is a deeper hunger for truth and contentment. My need for personal fulfillment is also unique to me and I do not expect she would feel the same way either. It has to be acknowledged. I am delighted she has never been a mommy pleaser – harder to parent at times, but she has an independent mind and she acts on it.

Much the same that many readers will resonate with the weight I put on this independence versus others, who are happy with a balance of compromise to live happy lives. My second chapter will require even more commitment to being brave because living can take more effort alone. Even though I remain fit and healthy through an active lifestyle, just getting up and doing things on my own with less than gazelle-like joints, AND maintaining a healthy dose of motivation, will be harder some days. I do not hide this fact from myself or my daughter. And I have reiterated to all my dear friends that I will be calling on them for much needed visits over the coming years. We're all in agreement that we will be emotionally supportive for each other in our fifties and beyond. It's optional for spouses, but as friends, we have grown to know each other resolutely and accept each other's flaws, weaknesses, and warts without reservation.

Bravery for me will continue with the way in which I seek to learn and embrace new things and how I thrive when I take deep breaths at the start of new adventures to push out my ribcage. The way in which I reflect on my life lessons and personal relationships to avoid very deep potholes going forward will say a lot about me. I don't plan to be alone for the rest of my older years but trying really hard not to commit to a companion for a few short years is important now. I am striving for a lifelong love, and why not.

Making an impact with people through my purposeful work, charitable and profitable, will keep me happily busy. Upon the completion of this book, I will seek to spend more time doing presentations and coaching people to identify what bravery feels and looks like for them. The task is to ensure everyone accepts we are genuinely different; we think differently and each person's appetite for life, and what we fill it with, will remain unique. Our legacies will be what we determine them to be and how we live to create them.

— **The End** —